Illusion, Disillusion, and Irony in Psychoanalysis

John Steiner

 Routledge
Taylor & Francis Group

LONDON AND NEW YORK

First published 2020
by Routledge
2 Park Square, Milton Park, Abingdon, Oxon OX14 4RN

and by Routledge
52 Vanderbilt Avenue, New York, NY 10017

Routledge is an imprint of the Taylor & Francis Group, an informa business

© 2020 John Steiner

British Library Cataloguing-in-Publication Data
A catalogue record for this book is available from the British Library

Library of Congress Cataloging-in-Publication Data
Names: Steiner, John, 1934- author. Title: Illusion, disillusion, and
irony in psychoanalysis / John Steiner.
Description: New York : Routledge, 2020. | Includes bibliographical
references and index.
Identifiers: LCCN 2019059185 (print) | LCCN 2019059186 (ebook) |
ISBN 9780367467029 (hardback) | ISBN 9780367467012 (paperback) |
ISBN 9781003030508 (ebook)
Subjects: LCSH: Psychoanalysis.
Classification: LCC BF173 .S678 2020 (print) | LCC BF173 (ebook) |
DDC 150.19/5–dc23
LC record available at https://lccn.loc.gov/2019059185
LC ebook record available at https://lccn.loc.gov/2019059186

ISBN: 978-0-367-46702-9 (hbk)
ISBN: 978-0-367-46701-2 (pbk)
ISBN: 978-1-003-03050-8 (ebk)

Typeset in Times
by Swales & Willis, Exeter, Devon, UK

Contents

Acknowledgements

I would like to thank the Melanie Klein Trust for their support and also the many colleagues who read drafts of the papers in the book: including Priscilla Roth, Ignes Sodre, and especially Susan Lawrence. The West Lodge annual conferences conducted together with Michael Feldman, Priscilla Roth, and Ron Britton have been a source of stimulation since their inception in 1995 and so too have been the discussions and clinical presentations in my postgraduate workshop. I would also like to thank Mary Block for her editorial help.

As usual my wife Deborah took an active part both as a wife and as a critical reader. She could no longer see well enough to read the manuscript but when I read the chapters to her, often several times over, she made many useful corrections and suggestions.

Credit lines

Reprinted by permission of the publisher (Taylor & Francis Ltd, www.tandf online.com):

Steiner, J. (2013). The Ideal and the Real in Klein and Milton: Some Obser vations on Reading Paradise Lost. *Psychoanalytic Quarterly*, 82: 897–923.

Steiner, J. (2015). The Use and Abuse of Omnipotence in the Journey of the Hero. *Psychoanalytic Quarterly*, 84: 695–718.

Steiner, J. (2016). Illusion, Disillusion, and Irony in Psychoanalysis. *Psycho analytic Quarterly*, 85: 427–447.

Steiner, J. (2018). Overcoming Obstacles in Analysis: Is It Possible to Relin quish Omnipotence and Accept Receptive Femininity? *Psychoanalytic Quarterly*, 87: 1–20.

Steiner, J. (2018). Overcoming Obstacles: Response to Rosemary H. Balsam. *Psychoanalytic Quarterly*, 87: 33–37.

Steiner, J. (2018). The Trauma and Disillusionment of Oedipus. *International Journal of Psychoanalysis*, 99: 555–568.

Steiner, J. (2018). Time and the Garden of Eden Illusion. *International Jour nal of Psychoanalysis*, 99: 1274–1287.

Steiner, J. (2020). Learning from Don Quixote. *International Journal of Psy choanalysis*, 101, 1–12.

Foreword

Jay Greenberg

In this volume John Steiner extends and develops the seminal ideas that he introduced in his classic *Psychic Retreats*. In that book, Steiner wrote about a particular group of patients who are generally considered difficult to treat. These deeply disturbed patients are unable to bear the pain of even minimal contact with reality, even with the therapists to whom they have turned for relief of their suffering. Because of this, they have withdrawn into the safety and the illusory satisfactions of elaborately constructed hiding places.

Steiner's probing, compassionate, and always nuanced suggestions for engaging these patients have guided a generation of analysts through some of the darkest moments in our working lives. And now, surprisingly and fortuitously for all of us, he has seen that what he described is more broadly true not only for patients but for all of us. The need to withdraw into a world of illusion, to create our own personal Garden of Eden is, he shows us, "precisely what many of our patients do and the same is true of course for all of us since we are all patients and all have serious problems with reality".

Some of these serious problems, Steiner shows us, are specific to individual lives and to suffering that has been imposed by the cruelty or neglect of others. The foundational myths of Western and others cultures speak eloquently to this and to the emotionally complex sequelae of brutal treatment. Oedipus, as Steiner notes, was a traumatised child, and the damage done to him was compounded because the people closest to him arranged, collusively if tacitly, to deny the effects of what was done to him.

But other serious problems are intrinsic and unavoidable aspects of the human condition. The facts of life that we deny when we retreat into illusions of Paradise "all involve a recognition of the passage of time. The shock of disillusion can be traumatic as time forces us to recognize first that all good things come to an end and ultimately that this includes life itself".

Because we are immersed in time that is inexorably moving forward, exposing us to the inescapably ephemeral nature of all that we love and to our own mortality, we are constantly challenged to come to terms with the limitations that, along with our potentials, define us. Another way of putting this is to say that we are always (although rarely consciously) engaged in a process of mourning. The challenge is to tolerate mourning, making it possible for us to work through our losses in a way that potentiates creative living.

In an image that runs through the book, Steiner describes the two expulsions that are the theme of Milton's *Paradise Lost*. Adam and Eve, mourning the loss of Eden and accepting both their humiliation and their guilt, are eventually able to embrace the possibilities of living in what has become their reality. The satisfactions of work, the joys of sex, even the beauties of living in a world that constantly changes may be felt as more deeply fulfilling than the effortless and static Paradise that they have left behind. Lucifer, in contrast, is unable to cope with any of the feelings stirred by the loss of his idealised relationship with God or with his banishment from Heaven. As a result the light goes out—literally from his name, which is changed to Satan—and from the world of darkness which he rules but in which he is eternally entrapped.

But Steiner is far too subtle and restless a thinker to be content with that account, or to be content with any single storyline. Accordingly, along with his growing appreciation of the role that illusion plays in all our lives in the years since he wrote *Psychic Retreats* he has come to a deeper appreciation of the ways in which illusion, while it can be pathological and defensive, is also indispensable. If they prevent us from fully enjoying the beauties of reality, including its transience, illusions also provide consolations and satisfactions that we all need some of the time. As a result, he is able to show that "periodically it is necessary to evade the truth and accept illusion", even though "for development to proceed we must return to face the truth about ourselves and about the world around us".

It would be a mistake, despite the developmental implications, to think of this as a process that moves forward in any way that we might consider linear. Nothing is simply linear in Steiner's vision; everything is both one thing and another, best appreciated by those of us who are capable of embracing an ironic vision. This applies both to our clinical work and to our lives outside the consulting room, and Steiner is a master at showing us that analytic process, for all its technical aspects, is always and foremost a meeting between two human beings, each of whom brings his or her own aspirations, struggles, and vulnerabilities to the encounter.

As a result, Steiner views the psychoanalytic situation with a depth and nuance that has always been rare in psychoanalytic discourse. It is not only patients who need or experience illusions, he writes, but analysts as well. And the analyst's illusions are not simply countertransferential in any conventional sense. Consider this: every time we enter the patient's mind through an act of sympathetic imagination we enjoy an illusion of closeness based on omnipotence, and every time we emerge to observe what we have been doing we have to face and mourn the loss of the illusion we have been enjoying.

Because the analyst by virtue of his or her humanity is as subject to illusion as everybody else, we must always be wary of just how we are influencing our analysands. In a wonderful subhead, Steiner talks about "The analyst as zealot", and reminds us that our illusions can distort our appreciation of the complexity of both analytic process and analytic change. With rare wisdom and humility, he reminds us that it is always difficult to distinguish between the patient's acceptance of reality and his or her submission to (analytic) authority; our personal illusions can lead us to turn a blind eye to this problem.

Our best safeguard, Steiner teaches, is to struggle to hold an ironic point of view, one that allows us simultaneously to empathise with our analysands and to observe them from our perspective as outsiders. We should adopt a similar perspective toward our own participation, he says. In a passage that could only be written by an analyst who has spent a lifetime grappling with the power and the vexations of our method he says: "an important safeguard in these cases arises from a sense of irony which constantly reminds us of something ridiculous and comic in our attitude and can thus act as a safeguard that prevents us from taking ourselves too seriously".

Although his choice to illustrate much of what he has to say using material from classic literary works to illustrate the universality of his view of illusion and disillusion, that is not the only or the most important determinant of the way Steiner engages the themes that run through the book. In his Introduction, he tells us that because of his retirement from clinical practice he has decided to turn to literature for his examples (he does, as I have noted, include a significant amount of clinical material, which is invariably both inspiring and illuminating). The choice to share his ideas about literature is a gift to his readers, because it gives us the chance to read some great works through his eyes; Steiner moves gracefully from Sophocles to Milton to Ibsen, Keats, Cervantes, Shakespeare, and many others. At each stop we find ourselves surprised and enlightened by the way he develops his theme in the context of works that are long familiar to us.

But alongside the depth and generosity of his reading we are aware throughout of his personal experience having made the choice to spend less time with examples from his practice. Steiner tells us, with the honesty and humility that runs throughout the book, that his choice "occasions some regret". Which of course it must, because it acknowledges that he is personally living what he is writing about, he is experiencing the passage of time and the loss of something that he loved and that inspired him for many decades.

The result is that at the same time as we learn from Steiner's insights, we get to experience at first hand his efforts to sustain creativity and passion even, and especially, as he experiences his own sense of what time has taken away. His decision to share his regret lends a depth and poignancy to all that he is teaching us. We feel Steiner's heart along with his brilliance on every page, and we as we share his journey we deepen our appreciation of the loss and the possibility that together give shape to our lives.

Introduction

A central theme, which is common to all of the chapters in this book, is that illusions are universal and ubiquitous. Their existence needs to be accepted, but eventually, if development is to proceed, they have to be recognised for what they are and a return to reality envisaged. Just as we need defences, we need illusions, but we also need to be able to emerge from the illusion and face reality. The conflict between the wish to evade and the wish to accept reality is an essential aspect of the human condition and it involves accepting both our strengths and our limitations. The acceptance of both illusion and reality requires an ability to entertain different contradictory attitudes and beliefs simultaneously and I will later discuss how this acceptance is facilitated if we are able to adopt an ironic stance.

Illusions can be thought of as states of mind to which we can withdraw, mostly to escape from various sources of anxiety and pain, but partly to enjoy the instant gratifications they provide. We evade uncomfortable aspects of reality replacing them with phantasies that provide us with comfort, reassurance and pleasure.[1] We can turn a blind eye to external dangers and we can also evade uncomfortable impulses arising from within. The defensive function of illusions allows them to be viewed as a particular version of a *psychic retreat* into which we can withdraw and enjoy an idealised alternative world. In this way the present book can be seen as a development of my earlier work on psychic retreats (Steiner, 1993, 2011), in which I wish to draw attention both to the previously studied function of psychic retreats as defensive systems but also to new considerations that arise from descriptions of ideal states on the one hand and the trauma of disillusion on the other.

The idealised illusions on which I focus attention play an important role in psychic life, sometimes as conscious beliefs of a blissful time that was once enjoyed and sometimes as unconscious phantasies of an idealised state which only becomes apparent following the trauma of disillusionment. Most of these states involve one version or another of a phantasy of a time as an infant at the breast when we enjoyed a total possession of the mother and were the sole recipients of her love. I refer to these phantasies as Garden of Eden Illusions and I suspect they will be familiar to most readers. Sometimes the analysis itself is idealised and sometimes it is denigrated by comparison with other relationships from which the analyst is excluded (Steiner, 2008). Less often recognised is the observation that the Garden of Eden Illusion forms the basis of many disturbing experiences in which disappointment and frustration arise because the promise of perfection fails to be delivered. Rage and hatred, both in the transference and outside it, commonly follow feelings of having been betrayed when the promise of perfections fails to materialise and the illusion is shattered by contacts with reality.

Clinical material is presented in three chapters, from Mr A in Chapters 5 and 7 and Mrs A in Chapter 6. Because of my retirement from analytic practice I have had to use material that has been published before but I hope it helps us to see the clinical relevance of the ideas I am exploring. In other chapters I have been encouraged to turn to examples from literature where many detailed descriptions of illusion and disillusion can be found. This shift occasions some regret but I have found that poets provide insights that are highly relevant for the psychoanalyst. It is important to note that my approach to these literary examples has been to view them with the eyes of a clinician, and not as a literary critic. I try to apply what I learn from them to the clinical situation and I presume that the analytic reader will be able to take the ideas back to his individual clinical environment and see to what extent he finds them to be useful. Of course, this is the case with clinical material in general and even when extensive and nearly verbatim sessions are presented the ideas have to be examined and tested through their application by others. Those readers who are not clinicians are left to evaluate the ideas through their own experience of life and of literature.

I start with the biblical myth of the expulsion from Eden and Milton's elaboration of it in *Paradise Lost* which has helped me to understand many aspects of idealised illusions. I am also indebted to Ibsen's *The Wild Duck*, Joseph Campbell's *Journey of a Hero*, and poetry by Keats and Shakespeare which enabled me to illustrate ideas of clinical relevance. Sophocles' Oedipus the King has been worked over from countless points of view by psychoanalysts and I justify the discussion here because of its relevance to my themes of illusion, disillusion, and irony.

Some patients believe that they once enjoyed a Garden of Eden state of perfection from which they were unjustly expelled and attempt to recreate such states in their everyday lives and, of course, in their analysis. Sometimes they believe they have been successful and descriptions of idealised families and idealised transference relationships are quite common, but more often the Garden of Eden Illusion is experienced in the form of a state which might have been, or should have been, enjoyed. Indeed, as the idealisation is shattered the feeling of having been unfairly expelled from Paradise is a common source of resentment and can give rise to a more paranoid psychic retreat based on grievance. Even then the Garden of Eden

Illusion plays an important role serving as an expectation against which current experience is judged.

We all need illusion to protect us from the impact of reality, from both the terrifying experience of life in its harshness and cruelty and from the equally frightening expressions of our internal thoughts and feelings. We also use illusions about our capacity to overcome obstacles in order to support adventures that we might realistically be daunted by. Without illusion life would at times be unbearable and at other times be unbearably dull and we need illusion to protect us from the need to face the truth about ourselves and about the world we live in and to ensure that we develop in an environment that is not overwhelmed by anxiety and depression.

This emphasis on illusion may seem strange coming from a psychoanalyst because we also profess that facing the truth is an important condition for mental health. Living in an unreal world deprives us of the pleasures and satisfactions that reality brings and the argument for the importance of illusion is relevant only as a temporary expedient. If development is to proceed we must sooner or later return to take account of the real world. Indeed, we gain strength from Freud's insistence that a respect for the truth is central to the analytic attitude.

> And finally we must not forget that the analytic relationship is *based on a love of truth*—that is, on a recognition of reality—and that it precludes any kind of sham or deceit.
>
> (Freud, 1937, p. 248)

Others have elaborated on the importance of truth and Bion even described it to be an essential nutrient of the mind just as food is to the body (1970). Dr Johnson, in the famous remarks quoted by Bion, asserts the solidity and durability of truth even though he acknowledges that it may not give us much consolation.

> Whether to see life as it is will give us much consolation, I know not; but the consolation which is drawn from truth, if any there be, is solid and durable; that which may be derived from error must be, like its original, fallacious and fugitive.
>
> (From a letter of Dr Johnson to Bennet Langdon quoted by Bion, 1970, p. 7)

It does seem that we need the consolations of illusion as well as the solidity and durability of truth. This was a point made by Winnicott who believed that the close attention of the mother to his needs made it easy for the infant to live in the illusion that he could control her with omnipotence.

> The mother, at the beginning, by an almost 100 per cent adaptation affords the infant the opportunity for the illusion that her breast is part

of the infant. It is, as it were, under the baby's magical control. The same can be said in terms of infant care in general, in the quiet times between excitements. Omnipotence is nearly a fact of experience. The mother's eventual task is gradually to disillusion the infant, but she has no hope of success unless at first she has been able to give sufficient opportunity for illusion.

(Winnicott, 1953, p. 95)

I suspect that the "almost 100 per cent adaptation" is itself an idealised illusion and only happens in phantasy but Winnicott's main point about the necessity for disillusion is central to my theme. I hope that the conclusion that will emerge from this book is that periodically it is necessary to evade the truth and accept illusion but that for development to proceed we must return to face the truth about ourselves and about the world around us. This means that the joys of illusion as well as the pains of disillusionment are recurring experiences as we journey through life.

The Garden of Eden Illusion

A particularly common and important illusion arises from a universal belief that we once experienced a blissful time that has tragically been lost and may magically be revived. The prototype for this ideal lies in the phantasy of a time of unlimited gratification as an infant at the breast in which the mother–baby couple had only each other to enjoy. As with every illusion the blissful time is eventually brought to an end with a more or less traumatic disillusionment which involves the recognition that the mother has an independence that challenges the belief in total possession. The disillusion may be linked to weaning or to the recognition of the birth of a real or imagined sibling but its essence is that the mother's mind lies outside the omnipotent control of the infant.

This universally held illusion has its counterpart in the mythological history of our culture where every age seems to have its Paradise. While the biblical story is perhaps the best known, similar myths exist in most cultures. Hesiod describes a Golden Age without sorrow, toil, and grief (Hesiod, 7 century BCE), echoed in the pastoral harmony of Arcadia where Pan enjoyed an unrestricted reign. The connection of these myths with the individual phantasy of bliss at the breast is confirmed by the idealised nature of many of the myths. This is vividly expressed in Cervantes' version of the Golden Age elaborated by Don Quixote as an idyllic time brought to a close with the shocking realisation of the parents' relationship and the potential advent of siblings.

Fortunate the age and fortunate the times called golden by the ancients ... because those who lived in that time did not know the two words *thine* and *mine*.

In that blessed age all things were owned in common; no one, for his daily sustenance, needed to do more than lift his hand and pluck it from the sturdy oaks.

...

In that time all was peace, friendship, and harmony; the heavy curve of the plowshare had not yet dared to open or violate the merciful womb of our first mother, for she, without being forced, offered up, everywhere across her broad and fertile bosom, whatever would satisfy, sustain, and delight the children who then possessed her.

(Cervantes, 1605a, Vol.1, Chapter II, p. 76)

Commenting on this version of the Garden of Eden Illusion which is explored in Chapter 9, I suggest that for Don Quixote the Golden Age is a phantasy of a pre-oedipal existence where the purity of the mother had not yet been violated, and involves an illusion of an idealised infant–mother couple.

The close relationship between mythological descriptions and those of individual experience enable us to consider the personal and clinical relevance of accounts such as those of Cervantes in Don Quixote and of Milton in *Paradise Lost*. It is particularly in the latter that the details of both the bliss of Paradise and the horrors of disillusion are presented with a beauty and emotional conviction that I find deeply moving and clinically relevant. They shed light on factors that affect individual patients and deepen our understanding of both infantile experience and its repetition in the transference.

The dual stance involved in the analytic attitude

The acceptance of illusion is an important aspect of the psychoanalytic attitude. As we listen to our patients we allow ourselves to be drawn into their story and we become identified with the patient's situation and join him in his phantasy world where we partake of his pleasures and his sorrows. We become involved in the patient's drama just as we become involved in the characters of a play we watch at the theatre or with the hero of a novel we are reading. This kind of participation involves the suspension of disbelief and the capacity to tolerate illusion, but eventually, of course, we need to detach ourselves in order to study the patient from the point of view of an observer, just as we think about the meaning of the play after we leave the theatre. It is then that we become aware of the disparity between the phantasy world which we have transiently been sharing and the real world that we wake up to and that ultimately we are obliged to accept.

In my discussion of this theme I describe Aristotle's proposal that the two emotions of terror and pity are typically evoked in tragic drama. In this context terror involves a fear of something happening to ourselves as we identify with the hero while pity arises as we withdraw from the identification and observe the suffering as it is happening—not to us, but to someone we have come to care about. The analyst suffers these and similar experiences as he listens to his patient and this can lead first to an empathic response and then to attempts to observe and create hypotheses as to what is going on. Eventually the empathic subjective sharing of an experience and the more objective attempt to observe from outside are combined to create a picture of what is going on between the patient and the analyst. The conclusions can give rise to hypotheses and these are in turn tested by interpretation followed by further participation and observation.

Irony and the analytic attitude

Irony is an important theme throughout this book and will be elaborated in detail in Chapter 10. However, it must be at least briefly mentioned here because the dual approach I have described is made more possible through a capacity for irony that enables opposing ideas and beliefs to be held simultaneously. With the help of irony the analyst can tolerate and indeed share the illusions brought by his patient and yet, for the most part, is able to extricate himself and retain his judgement based on a more objective view. The process is full of uncertainty and at several points in the book I reiterate the need to remember that our understanding is always tentative and requires testing, corroboration, and modification through further observations of the patient in the transference. I suggest that the capacity for healthy self-doubt is related to the capacity for irony which is a quality found in most serious writers and, as we shall see, is brilliantly portrayed by Sophocles, Shakespeare and Cervantes.

Paradise Lost

In view of Milton's literal belief in the reality of God, it may seem surprising to view *Paradise Lost* as a work of irony. However, a striking feature of the poem is the way it can encompass a variety of different views. While he justifies God as a symbol of absolute goodness Milton can also present him as an irritable and tyrannical autocrat. While Satan is presented as a symbol of absolute evil he is also sympathetically portrayed as someone treated with cruelty and injustice. Blake thought that Milton gave Satan the best lines, "because he was a true Poet and of the Devil's party without knowing it" (Blake, 1825–27 p. 6). Milton believed that it was necessary to "justify the ways of God to Men", precisely because he recognised that opposing views were possible. The poem is impressive in the way it induces contradictory interpretations, especially of God as a figure that can be hated as well as loved.

My initial interest in *Paradise Lost* arose from my concern with shame and humiliation that are so vividly portrayed in the experience of the expulsion from Eden (Steiner, 2006, 2011). The evident suffering is not just due to the loss of an ideal state but includes the sense of having done wrong and being discovered. It has always seemed to me to be a representation of the feelings of an infant emerging from an idealised place where he felt himself to be in possession of the breast, and with it of the mother's love, into a more reality based connection with the world in which the existence of others begins to impinge. Guilt is a feature but it is shame that initially dominates and this arises from the knowledge of being observed as small and needy, in a painful contrast with the earlier phase of omnipotent possession, which is now exposed as an illusion (Steiner, 2006, 2011).

There are many other clinical areas that the poem illuminates and despite the apparent gap between Milton's views and those of today, I was impressed by how little the difference of time and of outlook affects our capacity to appreciate the poem and to use the insights it offers. The idealised phantasies of Milton's Paradise are explored in Chapter 1 where I try to show how easy it is to become seduced by the idea of endless perfection. Initially we are drawn into the enjoyment of effortless gratification and the prohibition against eating of the fruit of the tree of knowledge seems a puzzling but unimportant limitation. As we step back however and consider what life would actually be like in Paradise we see that both the individual phantasy of perfection at the breast and the historical myth of a Garden of Eden prove to be ideal only if time is disregarded. In the real world perfection exists only in idyllic moments while in the Garden of Eden Illusion these moments are believed to be extended indefinitely. Moreover, life in the absence of time which at first seems so ideal soon reveals its drawbacks. If nothing changes, everything soon becomes uniform and boring. Adam and Eve are never hungry or cold and there are no memories of childhood and no feelings of regret or loss. Milton describes an idealised and rather passion-free sexual relationship but there is no aggression, no feelings of regret, and no longings. There is no violence and no killing because the animals peacefully coexist and even the pain and anxiety of childbirth is only mentioned after the fall. The endless pleasure creates an ideal of romantic perfection that seems attractive at first but soon pales and is revealed to be superficial and unsatisfying. Deeper emotions become liberated when Paradise is foregone and reality is faced outside of Eden. We realise that idealised and persecutory states have been kept apart through the mechanism of splitting which in the mythology of the Garden of Eden gives rise to a perfect Heaven and a persecutory Hell. Knowledge of good and evil involves recognising that both halves of the split have to exist and Satan is the necessary counterpart of God and has to be expelled if the perfection of Heaven is to be sustained. As well as the spatial version of the split between good and evil we see, when we take note of time, that splitting is also temporal and the early experience of the infant takes the form of idealised blissful states alternating with persecutory ones.

The terrible shock of expulsion from Paradise vividly connects to the experience of the baby when he no longer feels in possession of the ideal breast. Again we empathise with the awful disillusion that can seem so cruel and unjust until we step back and recognise that what is experienced as a punishment for disobedience is nothing more nor less than a return to reality. In the absence of illusion we live in a world in which the ordinary pleasures and pains of living have to be met. In Milton's account God sentences Adam and Eve to suffer the pains of childbirth, to the need to work for food, and to the necessity of facing his mortality in the inevitability of ageing and death. These facts of life that have been denied in Paradise all involve a recognition of the passage of time. The shock of disillusion can be traumatic as time forces us to recognise first that all good things come to an end and ultimately that this includes life itself.

Disillusion is further explored in Chapter 2 where the expulsion of Adam and Eve is compared with that of Lucifer. Adam and Eve eventually accept their fate and are able to mourn the loss of Paradise and with it the illusion of omnipotence that they had enjoyed. Such contrition is not possible for Lucifer who could not accept the humiliations inflicted on him by God. He was forced to submit to the realisation that he was not pre-eminent in God's favour and, with his band of angels, he rebelled to instigate the terrible war in Heaven that eventually led to his downfall and expulsion to Hell. Again Milton is in no doubt that the purity of Heaven had to be maintained and that evil had to be relegated to a separate kingdom but his sympathy with the suffering of Lucifer is clear. He describes how provoking it must have been when, seemingly out of the blue, Christ was introduced as God's favourite to whom all the angels were obliged to pay homage. It is an understanding of this mixture of sympathy combined with undeniable logic that is facilitated by a capacity for irony in which both attitudes can be entertained.

For Milton God was an ideal that could be internalised and serve as a model of perfection and for Klein the breast in its good aspects served a similar role.

> We find in the analysis of our patients that the breast in its good aspect is the prototype of maternal goodness, inexhaustible patience and generosity, as well as of creativeness. It is these phantasies and instinctual needs that so enrich the primal object that it remains the foundation for hope, trust and belief in goodness.
>
> (Klein, 1957, p. 180)

Milton repeatedly warns that the perfection of God is something denied to Man who has to face the gap between his own imperfect state and the ideal represented by God. In the case of Lucifer this gap proved to be intolerable leading him to mount his rebellion against God which is crushed with enormous cruelty as he is cast headlong into Hell.

> Him the Almighty Power
> Hurld headlong flaming from th' Ethereal Skie
> With hideous ruine and combustion down

To bottomless perdition, there to dwell
In Adamantine Chains and penal Fire,
Who durst defie th' Omnipotent to Arm.
                    (Book One, 49)

The critical issue is that of facing disillusion which is accepted by Adam and Eve who are able to relinquish their bliss and mourn the loss of Paradise, but not by Lucifer. He is unable to accept the loss of omnipotence and is obliged to live in his separate domain where he dedicates himself to a continual hatred of the goodness of God. Just as God comes to represent perfect goodness Lucifer, who is now renamed Satan, stands for perfect evil. Both these influences impinge on man who remains in a conflict between them that is never finally resolved. Both Milton and Klein describe how, as a result of accepting the loss, the ideal object is installed internally as a symbol that becomes a foundation for hope, trust and belief in goodness. This accords with the view that it is only if the loss of omnipotence can be faced that the good object can be mourned and transformed from its place as a concrete possession to be viewed as a symbol. The importance of this distinction between the real and the ideal becomes clear in relation to Garden of Eden Illusions in which the ideal becomes pathological when it ceases to function as a model of perfection and becomes a goal already achieved or a state that we are determined to restore.

The cruelty of truth

In Chapter 3 the dual stance taken by the analyst is explored in the relationship between the audience and the characters portrayed in Ibsen's great play, *The Wild Duck*. We enter into the drama initially accepting the importance of facing the truth but we are gradually made to see how reality can be brutal and traumatic. In the character of Gregers, Ibsen creates an advocate for the truth who ends up destroying the illusions that sustained the family of his friend Hialmar with tragic consequences. Eventually it becomes clear that Gregers has motives of his own that drive him towards righteous superiority and that his version of the truth is very partial.

Truth can be cruel in its unrelenting logic and it is easy for those who idealise truth to overlook the human limitations that make us depend on illusion in order to survive. This theme enables me to discuss the importance of kindness in the relationship between the observer and his object, and of course I am especially concerned with the clinical relationship between the analyst and his patient. I quote from E. M. Forster to suggest that kindness is important not simply to moderate the cruelty of truth but to make it more true. If truth is viewed from a rigid and narrow perspective we fail to recognise that it may be based on unconscious phantasies that are being denied. A wider truth can then emerge that includes an acceptance of human frailty, including our own. This raises the need to recognise when the pursuit of truth may make the analyst into a zealot in which a particular view of truth is idealised at the expense of the wider situation.

The journey of the hero

In Chapter 4 the *journey of the hero* is used to illustrate the importance of being able to espouse omnipotence in order to embark on dangerous ventures. Of course the hero has eventually to relinquish omnipotence and learn to respect reality if his adventures are to achieve real rewards but the ability and willingness to venture into unrealistic areas is necessary if advances are to be made. After all, what seems unrealistic to one generation can become real for subsequent ones. Omnipotence may also form the basis of the rebellion against conventional constraints that are necessary for new developments to proceed. A bid towards independence that overthrows established authority is unconsciously experienced as an oedipal murder and taking this path involves a painful working through of the heroic crime and its consequences.

In this chapter I make use of Joseph Campbell's famous and controversial ideas describing a universal structure to myths. He argues that myths commonly involve heroes who travel from the known world into the unknown where they face challenges and temptations, and engage in battles with superhuman forces. Eventually they face defeat and return with self-knowledge gained from the failure. I use the journey of the hero to emphasise both the need to be able to espouse omnipotence to break new ground and to relinquish it to return to reality in order for the achievement to be real.

An interesting link to personal development can be seen in Margaret Mahler's description of the stages of separation–individuation based on her observations of toddlers who enjoy a surge of omnipotence as they learn to walk. When the omnipotence fails, a collapse into shame and humiliation result in a clinging child in what she calls the rapprochement phase. Such experiences are common in the analytic situation and are similar to those I have described when patients begin to emerge from a psychic retreat based on omnipotence and have to survive the collapse of their self-importance. In this chapter the sequence is described in clinical material from a patient who at first defied reality in his ambitious adventures but began to make moves to work through the collapse and depression that followed disappointments to establish a more realistic and more gradual professional and personal development.

Disillusion, humiliation, and perversion of the facts of life

In Chapter 5, I describe how humiliation is always an element in disillusion and that it may become the focus of defensive manoeuvres that lead to perverse phantasies and mechanisms. Having lived in the illusion of perfection facing reality is always felt as a descent from a superior position and involves fears of being looked down on and despised. In order to deal with this and other aspects of emergence from Paradise the facts of life may be distorted, misrepresented and transformed into perverse scenarios. I describe what I think of as narcissistic perversions, oedipal perversions and perversions of the passage of time, each of which arise from one of Money-Kyrle's facts of life. Extracts from *Paradise Lost* are again used to argue that in one form or other phantasies of revenge and humiliation are universal responses to disillusion and make up a significant component of our erotic life.

The tragic repudiation of femininity

One of the tragic consequences of the Garden of Eden Illusion is that all of us whether male or female, turn to phantasies of phallic power in response to disillusion as a means of reversing feelings of smallness and dependence. This move is dominated by the immediate gratifications provided by phallic masculinity in the course of which femininity is disparaged and denigrated. The feminine in the form of the ideal breast is desired and even set on a pedestal to be admired but the means of possessing and controlling this desired object is based on power that is seen as masculine. Even when progress in analysis has led to a lessening of omnipotence it is sometimes surprising to find that development may continue to be blocked by persistent problems with femininity. It is not uncommon to find that relinquishing omnipotent solutions reminds us of our weakness and dependence which are persistently seen as inferior and feminine. I argue in Chapter 6 that these factors lead to a repudiation of femininity and a tendency to look down on women from a position of male superiority.

In "Analysis Terminable and Interminable" (1937), Freud identifies the repudiation of femininity as a major factor affecting our attitude to women and also creating obstacles to development and to progress in analysis. So great was the impasse that he believed it led to a bed-rock beyond which further progress was impossible. What Freud calls penis envy in women and a fear of a submissive attitude in men represents the same preference for a phallic masculinity that functions as a defence against what is felt to be an inferior and vulnerable feminine position. The reasons for this are complex but I suggest in this chapter that they are influenced by envy of a receptive femininity and a dread of a vulnerability to violent and often abusive phantasies associated with envy.

The capacity to identify and to dis-identify

I have described how we are inevitably drawn into the patient's drama as we engage with his account and empathise with his situation. While this empathy creates a feeling of companionship and understanding I also suggested that we need to dis-identify in order to return to our task of remaining separate to observe the patient as objectively as we can. Both these capacities are important and both play an important part in establishing an analytic attitude. Here again I argue that we can learn from artists and poets and in Chapter 7 I turn to look at Keats' extraordinary capacity to engage and identify with his objects. This is beautifully shown in his "Ode to a Nightingale" where he imagined that, like the nightingale, he was able to soar above the depression that reality inflicts. In an impressive flexibility of feeling he is also able to dis-identify with the nightingale and to return to face the truth of his condition with all of its pain. The specific reality that Keats is confronting is that of illness and death which is particularly moving when we recognise that he was to die from tuberculosis less than two years after writing the ode.

The relevance of empathic listening is illustrated with some clinical material where I try to show how important it is both to identify with the patient and to withdraw and attempt to view what has been happening from the position of a detached observer.

The role of trauma

Disillusion is subjectively felt as a trauma, as a punishment, and often as an injustice while to the observer it can seem to involve nothing more than giving up illusion to join with other mortals in the pleasures and pains of the real world. At other times the observer recognises that a trauma has been inflicted which involves more than just the relinquishment of an idealised phantasy. I look at this distinction in Chapter 8 where the effects of concrete physical trauma caused by parental neglect, violence, or abuse is examined. An often neglected example of such trauma is that which was inflicted on Oedipus, when as a baby his feet were pierced in order that he be exposed on a hillside and left to die. This enables a link to be made to those actual experiences of child abuse and neglect which I argue need to be taken into account by psychoanalysts when they try to understand traumatised patients. These cases are not rare and need to be differentiated from the situation that arises when the trauma consists chiefly of having to face the loss of an idealised illusion. When trauma is extreme the reality that has to be faced includes the idea that real damage has been done and that bad objects really do exist.

Oedipus suffered an actual trauma which was hidden beneath an idealised phantasy. He not only survived but grew up in a royal family which provided everything he needed except the truth of his origins. Like Adam and Eve his illusions could not survive the acquisition of knowledge and it was the revelation of the earlier evasions of truth that led to his downfall. I go on to suggest that actual trauma in the form of physical or mental abuse may make it more likely that a blissful psychic retreat is turned to as a defence and that this makes it more difficult to face the truth beneath the illusions.

The ingenious gentleman of La Mancha

In Chapter 9 I look at *Don Quixote*, one of the most celebrated works of irony in literature, again from the point of view of how it can help the analyst understand his attitude towards his patients. Cervantes provides us with wonderful comic entertainment but allows us to make contact with the underlying sadness and tragedy as he describes the countless ways that his hero tries to impose his day-dreams onto the world around him. The psychoanalyst can learn much about the complex relationships between phantasy and reality, the way illusion and insight can coexist and the way a vision of the ideal can sustain unreal goals. Here I draw attention to the shocking degree of violence, cruelty, and especially humiliation that is inflicted on the hapless knight. While at first Don Quixote's day-dreams are a source of amusement they provoke enormous cruelty when they impact on the lives of others. It is easy to label him as mad and then to mistreat him, and even his friends believe that they have licence to take over and control his life. I see this as a warning to the psychoanalyst who is placed in a special position of trust by the patient who inevitably feels vulnerable when he exposes his thoughts and allows himself to be observed. It is easy for the analyst to misuse this opportunity and to use his position to assume the superiority of his own beliefs.

Of course, the great beauty of the novel is the way irony is used to reconcile comedy with tragedy. We can laugh at the hero and at the same time love and pity him and also admire his noble vision.

The importance of irony

Finally, in Chapter 10 I explore the importance of irony to the understanding of our patients by examining its role in our response to Sophocles' *Oedipus the King*. This play is regularly used as the classic example of dramatic irony in which we identify with the actors on the stage who are ignorant of the truth and at the same time remain sufficiently detached as observers who can see and understand with knowledge that the heroes lack (Fowler, 1926). Irony enables more than one attitude to be entertained at the same time and facilitates an acceptance of illusion on the one hand and a respect for truth on the other. We have seen this in relation to the cruelty of truth in Ibsen's *The Wild Duck* in Chapter 3 and in Chapter 10 the dramatic irony of Oedipus' search for truth is re-examined with the help of an early paper on "Turning a blind eye", (Steiner, 1985). This enables me to argue that until the dramatic climax of the play Oedipus failed to pursue knowledge and was supported in this failure by the collusion of others both in the play and in the audience.

Throughout this book I have argued that it is the ironic attitude that allows us to adopt a humane response to the tragedies and comedies that we observe in the theatre as well as to those of our patients. It is a critical

element in the psychoanalytic attitude which enables us to give due attention both to phantasy and to reality, to truth and to kindness, and allows
us to relate to our patients with a sympathy based on shared experience.

Note

1 For simplicity I have used the spelling of phantasy with a "ph" rather than an
"f". Commonly "ph" has been used to refer to unconscious phantasy and "f" for
conscious fantasy. However, this distinction is often difficult to make and for my
purposes it is usually not important to differentiate between the two. I have also
used his and him when I hope it is clear that the point applies to both sexes, to
enable me to avoid the awkward him/her.

1   The Garden of Eden Illusion
Finding and losing Paradise[1]

Phantasies and daydreams of the ideal

In this opening chapter of a book on illusion and disillusion I am going to begin with a discussion of those unconscious phantasies of an ideal time of perfect pleasure and harmony that we all harbour and may not be aware of. The pervasive effects of such unconscious phantasies of perfection are often revealed through our discontents and grievances when it is recognised that the disappointment in what we have arises from a comparison with a perfection that unconsciously we believe we once possessed and then lost. Sometimes the phantasies emerge as conscious daydreams of heroic or romantic adventures which we all enjoy and can use to create an ideal world designed to satisfy every desire, but especially the desire to be loved and admired. Commonly the day-dreams are based on fairy-tales, novels, or films, in which we play the role of hero or heroine engaged in romantic adventures. While they vary in many of their details all such daydreams involve identifications with heroic figures and lead to wish-fulfilling adventures. It is not difficult to see that these phantasies are in part defensive and serve to reverse feelings of defeat and humiliation such as those that inevitably arise as we work through the Oedipus situation. In these wish-fulfilling daydreams the relationships tend to be romantic rather than explicitly erotic and the outcome implied rather than explicit. Later I will describe how the romance can turn nasty when the idealisation is thwarted and how a more sadistic scenario can become the vehicle for erotic excitement and perverse misrepresentations (see especially Chapter 6).

Most of us use romantic day-dreams only periodically, partly for the relief they provide and partly for the escapist pleasure they allow us to enjoy. Mostly they are recognised to be phantasies and they can be enjoyed as such even though we know that we have eventually to return to face the real world with its mixture of pleasures and pains. Sometimes, however, the phantasies come to take a concrete form where they are no longer daydreams but are treated as facts and are then no longer distinct from the real world which is expected to conform to the idealised expectations of Paradise. Such concretely held beliefs in the existence of perfection can seriously disturb development and lead to pathology.

The Garden of Eden Illusion

In many of these idyllic phantasies we can discern a reference to a Paradise that was once enjoyed and then tragically lost. The phantasies then emerge as attempts to undo or reverse the loss and to recreate the ideal state that is yearned for. The romantic scenarios can then be linked to the original romantic love affair of the baby with the mother and her breast, which is idealised as a blissful time of mutual admiration and exclusive love. The loss of perfection may then be experienced as a forcible expulsion often associated with humiliation which may then play a critical role in defensive responses.

Even those who recognise the idealisation as an illusion frequently retain an unconscious belief in the reality of a personal Paradise. Others believe that the ideal is a reality that they once enjoyed, often up to a particular moment when it all went wrong. These turning points are linked to the experience of weening but often identified with an event such as the birth of a sibling, a move of house, or the mother returning to work. It is especially in these cases of concrete belief that disillusion may be traumatic and give rise to powerful defences which can seriously disturb development. In an important paper anticipating this type of idealisation Akhtar (1996) described what he called "if-only" and "someday" phantasies in which nostalgia for the past and magical hopes for the future sustain the belief that the ideal state can be restored. They imply a failure of disillusionment which keeps a phantasy of an idealised state alive as one that might still be possessed, "if-only ..." the disillusion had not happened. They are often accompanied by the phantasy that "someday" it will all be magically put right and Paradise regained.

The phantasies may then function as idealised psychic retreats in which the patient becomes stuck to the detriment of development and growth. Even more disturbing are phantasies in which grievance turns to revenge and the good object is attacked for failing to deliver the desired perfection. A sense of entitlement can lead to a passionate striving for the promised ideal which is sometimes ruthlessly pursued and which may lead to political or religious fundamentalism in pursuit of utopian dreams.

The Garden of Eden in mythology

Individual Garden of Eden phantasies have their counterpart in the mythological history of our culture where every age seems to have its Paradise. Indeed, the German poet Schiller argued that all cultures have a Paradise in their history and that this corresponds to the Paradise that every individual remembers (Schiller, 1759–1805).

While the biblical story of the Garden of Eden is perhaps the best-known myth, many others refer to an ideal time once enjoyed and eventually lost. In Greek mythology the Golden Age of Hesiod describes how

> Men lived like gods without sorrow of heart, remote and free from toil and grief: miserable age rested not on them; but with legs and arms

never failing they made merry with feasting beyond the reach of all devils. When they died, it was as though they were overcome with sleep, and they had all good things; for the fruitful earth unforced bare them fruit abundantly and without stint. They dwelt in ease and peace.

(Hesiod, 7 century BCE)

Closely related is the version of Paradise referred to as Arcadia, an area in the Peloponnese of pastoral harmony where Pan enjoyed an unrestricted reign. The romantic images of beautiful nymphs frolicking in lush forests is presented as the spontaneous result of life lived naturally, uncorrupted by civilisation. Don Quixote's version of the Golden Age which is discussed in Chapter 10 is an ironic elaboration of the perfection of a time before the unlimited abundance of Paradise was challenged by the existence of Oedipal rivals.

Milton's Garden of Eden

In this chapter I am going to use extracts from Milton's *Paradise Lost* as well as some quotations from Keats together with Freud's paper "On Transience",[2] to discuss these idealised states as they appear in our personal history, I will suggest that their appearance in the phantasy life of the individual has similar features to those found in the myths and that in both the idealisation depends on a denial of the passage of time.

Milton's description of the Garden of Eden allows us to see that the ideal is particularly concerned with the abundance of food and the absence of delays and frustrations.

> A happy rural seat of various view;
> Groves whose rich Trees wept odorous Gumms and Balme,
> Others whose fruit burnisht with Golden Rinde
> Hung amiable, ...
> Flours of all hue, and without Thorn the Rose:
> .... umbrageous Grots and Caves
> Of coole recess, o're which the mantling vine
> Layes forth her purple Grape, and gently creeps
> Luxuriant ...
>
> (Book Four, 260)

All kinds of animals abound in peaceful harmony and among all this perfection Adam and Eve stand out as most perfect of all:

> Of living Creatures new to sight and strange:
> Two of far nobler shape erect and tall,
> Godlike erect, with native Honour clad
> In naked Majestie seemd Lords of all ...
>
> (Book Four, 290)

Work was not necessary and Adam and Eve did only so much labour as would whet their appetite.

> More grateful, to thir Supper Fruits they fell,
> Nectarine Fruits which the compliant boughes
> Yielded them, side-long as they sat recline
> On the soft downie Bank damaskt with flours:
> The savourie pulp they chew, and in the rinde
> Still as they thirsted scoop the brimming stream ...
>
> (Book Four, 336)

Around them the peaceful world in which the animals played meant that there was no violence, no strife, and no death.

> About them frisking playd
> All Beasts of th' Earth, since wilde, and of all chase
> In Wood or Wilderness, Forrest or Den;
> Sporting the Lion rampd, and in his paw
> Dandl'd the Kid; Bears, Tygers, Ounces, Pards
> Gambold before them, th' unwieldy Elephant
> To make them mirth us'd all his might, and wreathd
> His Lithe Proboscis;
>
> (Book Four, 347)

Perhaps most enviable was the idyllic relationship between Adam and Eve as they lay "imparadised" in one another's arms. This is Eve speaking:

> with that thy gentle hand
> Seisd mine, I yielded, and from that time see
> How beauty is excelld by manly grace
> And wisdom, which alone is truly fair.
> So spake our general Mother, and with eyes
> Of conjugal attraction unreprov'd,
> And meek surrender, half imbracing leand
> On our first Father, half her swelling Breast Naked met his under the
>   flowing Gold
> Of her loose tresses hid: he in delight
> Both of her Beauty and submissive Charms
> Smil'd with superior Love, as Jupiter
> On Juno smiles, when he impregns the Clouds That shed May Flowers;
>   and press'd her Matron lip
> With kisses pure: ...
>
> (Book Four, 500)

Of course, emphasising the woman's submissive charms is a male view of Paradise but one that is derived from infantile longings for a submissive mother. This is part of the infantile Garden of Eden Illusion of a blissful time when unlimited access to the breast was enjoyed without interference from siblings or fathers. Of course from the point of view of an analytic observer such phantasies are illusions and we recognise that, except for brief moments, no infantile situation is actually ideal.

The mechanism of splitting: spatial and temporal

From the point of view of the analytically trained observer idealised states create a misrepresentation of reality in which good and bad experiences are kept artificially separate through the mechanism of splitting. From the spatial point of view peace can only reign in the Garden of Eden, and indeed in Heaven, if everything bad is expelled and located in Hell. Satan's appearance introduces the idea that envy and hatred are part of the human condition and that the world is a mixture of good and bad elements but this cannot be tolerated because it threatens the idealisation. Vigorous attempts have to be made to expel Satan back to Hell where he belongs, in order to protect Adam and Eve and to restore the idealisation.

However, the split is also temporal and this leads to idealised and persecutory states that follow each other without any connection being made between them. Until integration becomes possible at a later stage of development the infant finds himself either in a state of idealisation or in one of persecution. Indeed, the shifts between these states are themselves only apparent to an observer because the subject is himself only aware of the current state he is in. Temporal integration requires memory to bridge the two experiences and the bridge has to take account of the passage of time. The idealised phantasy is ideal when it goes on for ever and when good experiences come to an end we are faced with loss and all its pain. Ultimately an awareness of time heralds the recognition of ageing and death and challenges the phantasy of immortality so central to the Garden of Eden Illusion.

The timeless nature of the Garden of Eden Illusion

Even a cursory consideration of what life is actually like in Paradise reveals it to be far from ideal. Both the individual phantasy of perfection at the breast and the historical myth of a Garden of Eden prove to be ideal only if time is disregarded. Indeed, the attraction of the ideal stems largely from the provision of an abundance which assures that there is no need to wait, no frustration and no anxiety. Perfect moments are experienced in all but the worst of circumstances but over time these alternate with periods that are far from perfect. The belief in an exclusive relationship with the mother, for example, depends on an illusion that what seems perfect now will go on forever and that the mother will never be distracted to attend to a sibling nor to her own internal and external relations.

If we imagine ourselves in the Garden of Eden the absence of time which at first seems so ideal, soon reveals its drawbacks. If nothing changes, life soon becomes uniform and boring. Adam and Eve are never hungry or cold and having been brought fully adult into Eden the pleasures of development and growing up are denied to them. There are no memories of childhood, no feelings of regret or loss. Fruit is always ripe and there are no seasons, no wilting of leaves, and no green shoots to look forward to, since neither decay nor regeneration takes place. Adam and Eve were ordered to procreate but pregnancy and childbirth seem to have been postponed and because the animals peacefully coexist their diet is vegetarian. The endless pleasure creates an ideal of romantic perfection that seems attractive at first but soon palls and is revealed to be superficial and unsatisfying. Deeper emotions become liberated when Paradise is foregone and reality is faced outside Eden.

Clinical material to support such observations has been reported by Heinz Weiss (2008), whose patient invited him to join her in a timeless world that was romantic, idealised, and erotised. If he failed to join in, the idealised world collapsed and the romance was turned into endless suffering which was also erotised, static, and timeless. He concluded that his patient created a *psychic retreat* in which the reality of time was misrepresented and perverted.

Time in Keats' Ode to a Grecian Urn

The timelessness of the ideal is captured in Keats' Ode to a Grecian Urn (Keats, 1819), which presents a scene of timeless perfection.

> Fair youth, beneath the trees, thou canst not leave
> Thy song, nor ever can those trees be bare;
> Bold Lover, never, never canst thou kiss,
> Though winning near the goal yet, do not grieve;
> She cannot fade, though thou hast not thy bliss,
> For ever wilt thou love, and she be fair!
> Ah, happy, happy boughs! that cannot shed
> Your leaves, nor ever bid the Spring adieu;
> And, happy melodist, unwearied,
> For ever piping songs for ever new;
> More happy love! more happy, happy love!
> For ever warm and still to be enjoy'd,
> For ever panting, and for ever young.

Such moments are possible in pictorial art and this contrasts with the case in music which requires movement in time. In his Ode to a Nightingale (Keats, 1819) which is discussed in Chapter 8, Keats illustrates how through music a continuity over time establishes duration and consequently brings us in touch with endings, mourning and loss. By contrast the painting on the Urn depicts lovers about to kiss and presents us with a snapshot in which time stands still.

When she wrote about this ode Ignes Sodre (2013) suggested that the poem was about the idealisation of timelessness. For the perpetuation of the fiction it is essential that ideal, romantic love must never be consummated. In the timeless idealisation, nothing changes and the images can remain ideal as a phantasy of a special moment before we have to face reality and time indicating that good things come to an end. Eventually accepting time means accepting the reality of ageing and death which Keats alludes to at the end of the ode:

> When old age shall this generation waste,
> Thou shalt remain, in midst of other woe
> Than ours, a friend to man, to whom thou say'st,
> "Beauty is truth, truth beauty,—that is all
> Ye know on earth, and all ye need to know".

Keats seems to be saying that the ideal is an illusion, but one that "in the midst of other woe" can be a consolation. In reality truth cannot be equated with beauty since we know that beauty will fade and much that is true is ugly. However, when time stands still Keats' statement is true and for that ideal moment truth and beauty are equivalent.

Rilke and Freud

In his short paper entitled "On Transience", Freud (1916) reported a discussion on a summer walk with "a poet and taciturn friend", later identified as Rilke and Lou Andreas Salome. Freud tried to challenge the poet's pessimistic view that he could see no value in beautiful things because he was so aware that they were fated to be lost. Spring could not be enjoyed because it will vanish when winter comes, and the same applied to all of the creations of man which cannot last forever.

Rilke seemed so distressed by loss that he could neither enjoy an ideal moment where time stands still nor subsequently relinquish it and face the loss. Freud suggested that, for Rilke, only immortality could give achievement value, and that this belief revealed a "revolt against the pain of mourning". For Freud, the fact that beauty was transient enhanced the value of the moment, as it did for Keats, but this was true only if the object of previous losses had been relinquished and mourned. The lost object could survive as an idea, as a memory, or as a phantasy, but only if the concrete illusion that it could be possessed forever was given up.

The scientist's concept of time

We are so embedded in an experience of time that it is difficult for us to know how to react when we are told that there was a time before time began. Stephen Hawking (1996) explains that the universe has not existed forever and that time itself had a beginning in the Big Bang, about 15.3 billion years ago. Perhaps it is equally difficult to imagine that the same is true for each one of us before we are born and after we die. A child sometimes asks, "Where was I before I was born?" We sustain an illusion of continuity when we imagine that we can continue to exist in our work or in our children. This is a common enough phantasy especially among poets, epitomised by Shakespeare when he claimed that:

> Not marble, nor the gilded monuments
> Of princes, shall outlive this powerful rhyme.
> (Sonnet 55)

However even the durability of Homer or Shakespeare involves a relatively short time scale in the long term scheme of the ages. It is nevertheless enriching to think that creative acts can be both lost and rediscovered and that transience need not detract from the value of what we have.

Love before and after the fall

We have seen how Milton's description of love-making before the fall is idyllic but rather bland. We are made aware that it is Satan who is observing this idyllic tableau and he is the one with intense feelings of rage, exclusion, and envy. The absence of passion in such ideal love is in sharp contrast to the feverish love-making after the fall.

> As with new Wine intoxicated both
> They swim in mirth, and fansie that they feel
> Divinitie within them breeding wings
> …
> Carnal desire enflaming, hee on Eve
> Began to cast lascivious Eyes, she him
> As wantonly repaid; in Lust they burne:
> Till Adam thus 'gan Eve to dalliance move,
> For never did thy Beautie since the day
> I saw thee first and wedded thee, adorn'd
> With all perfections, so enflame my sense
> With ardor to enjoy thee, fairer now
> Then ever, bountie of this vertuous Tree.
> So said he, and forbore not glance or toy
> Of amorous intent, well understood
> Of Eve, whose Eye darted contagious Fire.
> Her hand he seis'd, and to a shadie bank,
> Thick overhead with verdant roof imbowr'd
> He led her nothing loath;

Flours were the Couch, Pansies, and Violets, and Asphodel,
And Hyacinth, Earths freshest softest lap.

(Book Nine, 1044)

"Divinitie within them breeding wings", suggests that in their passion Adam and Eve have identified with God's omnipotence as, in their disobedience, the forbidden fruit has enlivened them towards a passionate sexuality.

As if to confirm that time does not exist the love-making before the fall has no consequences while after the fall things are very different and Adam and Eve, when they awake, are consumed with guilt and shame as they face the consequences of their disobedience. A capacity to experience time means that uncomfortable feelings are no longer split off into another world, but reside within the couple where they can eventually be accepted as part of the human condition. When we tolerate and accept the reality of time our innocence is permanently lost and the terrible realisation of the imperfections of human nature can be faced with tolerance and kindness.

Love in the real world is expressed with ambivalence having an admixture of aggression that gives rise to guilt. When time is taken to work through the consequences, the guilt can lead to reparative wishes which then combines with libidinal impulses to create a deeper and more convincing expression of love. Klein has expressed this deeper and more complex love as follows:

> I hold the view that feelings of sorrow, guilt and anxiety are experienced by the infant when he comes to realize to a certain extent, that his loved object is the same as the one he hates and has attacked and is going on attacking in his uncontrollable sadism and greed, and that sorrow, guilt and anxiety are part and parcel of the complex relation to objects which we call love. It is from these conflicts that the drive to reparation springs, which is not only a powerful motive for sublimations, but also is inherent in feelings of love, which it influences both in quality and quantity.
>
> (Klein, 2017, p. 12)[3]

The implication is that libidinal feelings are important but superficial until they become deepened by an awareness of the sorrow we feel when we hurt our good objects.

Milton seems to recognise this very theme when towards the end of the poem Christ describes man's contrition to God and argues that when goodness is released in the aftermath of rebellion it is deeper than that associated with dutiful obedience.

See Father, what first fruits on Earth are sprung
From thy implanted Grace in Man, these Sighs

And Prayers, which in this Golden Censer, mixt
With Incense, I thy Priest before thee bring,
Fruits of more pleasing savour from thy seed
Sow'n with contrition in his heart, then those
Which his own hand manuring all the Trees
Of Paradise could have produc't, ere fall'n
From innocence.

(Book Eleven, 30)

This theme seems to me to suggest that Milton recognised that Paradise had to be lost and mourned before deeper feelings of love could be discovered.

Seeing the world as it is: introducing time, work, love, and death

Of course, the deeper satisfactions of seeing the world as it is are durable and enriching but after the shock of disillusion it takes some time for these satisfactions to be realised. From the famous opening stanza Milton presents the act of disobedience as a disaster that might have been avoided and, at least for the righteous, it will one day be reversed.

Of Mans First Disobedience, and the Fruit
Of that Forbidden Tree, whose mortal taste
Brought Death into the World, and all our woe,
With loss of Eden, till one greater Man
Restore us, and regain the blissful Seat,
Sing Heav'nly Muse.

(Book One, 1–6)

Milton believed in the conventional view that the fall was a tragedy and "if-only" the seductions of Satan had been resisted Paradise might still be enjoyed. Moreover, he also subscribes to the "someday" phantasy that Paradise will be regained when a greater man restores us to the blissful seat. It is very difficult to relinquish such utopian beliefs which are held by most religious and political idealists and are probably held at an unconscious level by most of us. Adam and Eve initially share the view that their fate was terrible as was that of Lucifer when he was "*Hurld headlong flaming from th' Ethereal Skie*" into eternal Hell. Initially the reader shares this view but it is Milton's genius to allow us to take a closer look at God's severity and to recognise that Adam and Eve are sentenced to nothing more nor less than to live in the real world (Segal, 2007).

God announces their fate as follows.
And to the Woman thus his Sentence turn'd.
Thy sorrow I will greatly multiplie
By thy Conception; Children thou shalt bring

> In sorrow forth, and to thy Husband's will
> Thine shall submit, hee over thee shall rule.
>> (Book Ten, 195)

For Eve this meant enduring the pain of childbirth and submitting to man's superiority. We note in passing that Milton saw the submissive role of women to be ordained by God and although this will justifiably raise some hackles today, it points to the prevalent prejudices that see femininity as inferior (see the discussion of the repudiation of femininity in Chapter 6).

For Adam, God stressed that work would be arduous and its rewards hard-won.

> On Adam last thus judgement he pronounc'd ...
> Curs'd is the ground for thy sake, thou in sorrow
> Shalt eate thereof all the days of thy Life;
> Thorns also and Thistles it shall bring thee forth
> Unbid, and thou shalt eate th' Herb of th' Field,
> In the sweat of thy Face shalt thou eat Bread,
> Till thou return unto the ground, for thou
> Out of the ground wast taken, know thy Birth,
> For dust thou art, and shalt to dust returne.
>> (Book Ten, 207)

For both Adam and Eve their fate involved an introduction to time which will ultimately lead to the anticipation of ageing, illness, and death. These three elements, namely the need to work, to procreate, and eventually to die are perhaps the most basic aspects of reality that distinguishes life before and after the Fall. They remind us that we have these elements in common with all living creatures and they emphasise the fact that we are not omnipotent. We must submit to the reality of time and it is this that most significantly differentiates us from the omnipotence of the Gods.

Of these three elements Freud stressed two, namely the capacity to love and to work,[4] but, as his comments on transience confirm, he was acutely aware of our need to face ageing and death. Using different definitions but essentially referring to similar themes, these three elements were also singled out by Money-Kyrle (1968, 1971) as the three essential facts of life. It is these facts, which are discussed in detail in Chapter 6, that have an immediate impact when the illusion of perfection is shattered and each of them introduces the reality of time.

The value of reality and the importance of illusion

The enjoyment of our capacity to love and to work, requires at least a partial acceptance of reality and the analyst often finds himself trying to promote the advantages of reality to a reluctant patient. These advantages are substantial and we gain strength from Freud's insistence that a respect for the truth is central to the analytic attitude.

> And finally we must not forget that the analytic relationship is *based on a love of truth*—that is, on a recognition of reality—and that it precludes any kind of sham or deceit.
>
> (Freud, 1937, p. 248)

Klein echoed this view when she suggested that psychoanalytic technique is based on a prioritising of truth.

> If the urge to explore is coupled with *an unfailing desire to ascertain the truth*, no matter what this may be, and anxiety does not interfere too much with it, we should be able to note undisturbed what the patient's mind presents to us, irrespective even of the ultimate purpose of our work, namely, the cure of the patient.
>
> (Steiner, 2017, p. 29)

Bion (1970) described truth as an essential nutrient of the mind just as food is to the body and his quotation from Dr Johnson stresses the durability over time of the value of reality.

> Whether to see life as it is will give us much consolation, I know not; but the consolation which is drawn from truth, if any there be, is solid and durable; that which may be derived from error must be, like its original, fallacious and fugitive.
>
> (From a letter of Dr Johnson to Bennet Langdon)

Despite these assertions we are also aware of the importance of tolerating illusion, a theme stressed by Winnicott who suggested that until the infant is ready to face reality he and the mother come to an agreement never to question whether a belief is based on reality or illusion.

> Of the transitional object it can be said that it is a matter of agreement between us and the baby that we will never ask the question: "Did you conceive of this or was it presented to you from without?" The important point is that no decision on this point is expected. The question is not to be formulated.
>
> (Winnicott, 1953, p. 95)

Winnicott himself recognised that, ultimately, disillusion must be faced and that it is part of the mother's task to support her child as he faces reality rather than to continue to evade it.

The mother's eventual task is gradually to disillusion the infant, but she has no hope of success unless at first she has been able to give sufficient opportunity for illusion.

(Winnicott, 1953, p. 95)

Even Klein, who is often thought of as a champion of truth, recognised the value of illusion and believed that the idealised good object that is created by primal splitting assists in the internalisation of a good object.

We find in the analysis of our patients that the breast in its good aspect is the prototype of maternal goodness, inexhaustible patience and generosity, as well as of creativeness. It is these phantasies and instinctual needs that so enrich the primal object that it remains the foundation for hope, trust and belief in goodness.

(Klein, 1957, p. 180)

This is the ideal breast created by primal splitting and clearly giving rise to an illusion of perfection by being kept apart from the bad breast. Klein clearly sees this period of illusion to favour development until such time as the infant is strong enough to integrate the two sides of the split into a picture of the mother as she really is.

I believe that illusion must both be tolerated and also relinquished and in Chapter 4 I liken the individual development of the infant to the journey of the hero and argue that the infant must be able to espouse omnipotence and enjoy illusions in order to explore new worlds. However, to make these achievements real he must subsequently relinquish omnipotence and come back to earth. Without illusions our imaginative capacity would be restricted and artistic creativity would be confined to the mundane but without a return to reality the creativity of the imagination would remain illusory. Segal (1954, 1972) has suggested that it is his craft that links the artist to reality and transforms the achievements of the imagination into a concrete object that can be shared with others.

Collusion with family members that sustains the idealisation

Other members of the family are often surprisingly tolerant of the idealised mother–baby couple and manage to repress or control the envy and jealousy of the ideal couple that may later emerge with great force. We all agree that the new baby is perfect and we seem to take pride in owning the new arrival as *our* baby. Freud described this in relation to the narcissistic needs of the parents.

Thus they are under a compulsion to ascribe every perfection to the child—which sober observation would find no occasion to do—and to conceal and forget all his shortcomings ... the laws of nature and of society shall be abrogated in his favour; he shall once more really be the centre and core of creation—"His Majesty the Baby".

(Freud, 1914, p. 91)

Perhaps most remarkable is the almost universal observation that mothers idealise their babies. We see them earnestly telling their little hero that he is as strong as a lion and their little girl that she is the most beautiful in the world. Deborah Steiner has described how some infants are probably seduced into a *folie à deux* by such stimulation of their narcissism (Steiner, 2011), but most can find a degree of irony with which to interpret the meaning of the praise. They recognise that most mothers idealise their babies and that this is no more than a phase that will gradually yield to the influence of reality. Mothers and other members of the family conveniently forget the difficult times when the screaming baby can seem to be inconsolable.

How real is the illusion?

A number of writers, beginning with Freud, have argued that the idealised time of infancy may actually have been experienced as such because of the close attention provided by the caring mother. This is a time when the pleasure principle reigns and even though the idealisation is a fiction Freud nevertheless sees it as approximating real experiences.

> The employment of a fiction like this is, however, justified when one considers that the infant—provided one includes with it the care it receives from its mother—does almost realize a psychical system of this kind.
>
> (Freud, 1911, p. 219)

Making a similar point Winnicott (1953) describes how this almost 100 per cent gratification of the infant's desires supports the phantasy of omnipotent control.

> The mother, at the beginning, by an almost 100 per cent adaptation affords the infant the opportunity for the illusion that her breast is part of the infant. It is, as it were, under the baby's magical control. The same can be said in terms of infant care in general, in the quiet times between excitements. Omnipotence is nearly a fact of experience.
>
> (Winnicott, 1953, p. 94)

Sometimes the Garden of Eden Illusion extends to phantasies of life in the maternal womb which can be thought of as ideal. Thus Ferenczi describes intra-uterine life as "subservient only to pleasure".

> and that does so not only in imagination and approximately, but in actual fact and completely. ... all its needs for protection, warmth, and

nourishment are assured by the mother. ... [and] he must get from his existence the impression that he is in fact omnipotent. For what is omnipotence? The feeling that one has all that one wants, and that one has nothing left to wish for.

(Ferenczi, 1913, pp. 218–219)

The ease with which we impose our idealised phantasies on the patient's situation becomes clear when we examine what life is actually like in the womb. Some years ago an exhibit in the Natural History Museum allowed the visitor to enter a model of a womb which turned out to be a noisy place. The mother's breathing, heartbeat, and bowel sounds were far from tranquil and emphasised the vulnerability of the growing foetus. Moreover, the mother's heartbeat and breathing are not controlled by the infant's omnipotence but increase when she runs to catch a bus for example. Even the increase in nutrients in the umbilical cord occur when the mother decides to have a meal and are unrelated to the desires of the foetus.

The observer's tendency to share the idealised illusions of the Garden of Eden makes it easy to support the belief held by many patients, and perhaps at some level by all of us, that the idealised times actually did exist.

Illusion and symbolic function

When a concrete belief in the existence of the ideal is relinquished it continues to exist and to play an important role as a symbol of the ideal. The transformation of a fact into a symbol is a complex process which I discuss in Chapter 4 where I compare Milton's view of God as a symbol of perfect goodness with Klein's view of the ideal breast having an identical function. I suggest that a gap develops between the ideal as a symbol or aspiration and the ideal as a realisable achievement. I argue that this gap, which is also apparent in the difference between the ideal ego and the ego ideal creates problems in development where there is always a temptation to turn to solutions that are immediate and omnipotent. If time can be tolerated then mourning the loss of the ideal can be worked through and symbolic function can take development forward.

Persecutory retreats

It must be remembered that reality may be difficult to accept and this is particularly the case if the belief in the reality of the illusion is concrete and disillusion has been sudden and brutal. The child may then feel that like Lucifer, as he was thrown into an abyss of persecution.

Him the Almighty Power
Hurld headlong flaming from th' Ethereal Skie
With hideous ruine and combustion down

> To bottomless perdition, there to dwell
> In Adamantine Chains and penal Fire,
> Who durst defie th' Omnipotent to Arm.
>
> (Book One, 49)

Lucifer's fall evokes the image of an infant who is abruptly disillusioned after he believed that he was secure as the idealised favourite of the mother. Most commonly the disillusion arises as he is confronted with the reality of a third object in the Oedipal triangle. A new baby is announced and the infant feels thrown out from his unique place in which he lived in the illusion that the breast was his possession. He feels displaced from a Paradise, in which he can merge with the ideal object, "I'm the breast and the breast is me", to a position of separateness in which he feels that, "I need the breast, which is not me" (Freud, 1941). This often seems to lead to a realisation that "it is not uniquely mine either", which may be equated with the conviction that "I am not loved at all" (Sodre, 2008, 2012).

Lucifer was dethroned from the belief that his place in Heaven was second only to God as the *"First Arch-Angel, great in Power/In favour and præeminence"*, and he could not accommodate to the new situation. When he realised that God's love was not uniquely his he was deeply humiliated and when he could not be persuaded that he was still loved, he could not relent and was hurled headlong into chaos. Ultimately when he recovered from the shock his reaction was to create a psychotic organisation out of his corner of chaos and to reverse the humiliation by trying to defeat God in a struggle over power (Segal, 2007), claiming that it is, "Better to rule in Hell than serve in Heaven".

The awful dilemma that Satan finds himself in when he feels unable to repent and hence unable to make his peace with God is rendered more poignant when Milton describes him as wavering.

> Is there no place
> Left for Repentance, none for Pardon left?
> None left but by submission; and that word
> Disdain forbids me …

In sadness however he realises that there is no way back and it is this that leads him to espouse evil as his goal.

> So farewel Hope, and with Hope farewel Fear,
> Farewel Remorse: all Good to me is lost;
> Evil be thou my Good.
>
> (Book One, 110)

These descriptions seem to me to reflect the awful situation of the infant whose illusions of a perfect and exclusive relationship with the mother have been shattered. He feels, like Satan, that he has been expelled from the family because in his illusion of omnipotence he has challenged the authority of the father and that there is no way back. Having enjoyed the bliss of Paradise he now feels small and humiliated when it is exposed as an illusion. Sodre (2012) has suggested that normally the mother's love saves the day because it creates a link and is felt to rescue the baby from the abyss. In favourable circumstances the infant can recover from the disillusionment and use the experience to recognise a separateness between the self and the object. The object may then be seen more realistically and when it is no longer an idealised possession, a more realistic place in the family can develop in which the infant can accept a place as *one of* the objects of the mother's love rather than *the* object of her love. However, when this is not possible and the pain, humiliation, and fear are unbearable, a gap opens up between the self and the object; a gap that to start with is filled by Chaos, leading to panicky feelings of falling into a terrifying unknown. This means that the "horizontal" gap, between self and breast becomes a "vertical" gap, with only two positions, triumph or humiliation. The longing for love is then replaced by a longing for power. The patient inhabits an up or down universe in which strength fuelled by hatred is idealised and love is seen as weak and contemptible. It was in this kind of situation that Lucifer gave up the quest to be loved and dedicated himself to Evil. The patient may find himself like Satan, trapped in a persecutory psychic retreat in which the desire for revenge replaces the desire to be loved. The manner in which the disillusionment of ideal phantasies can lead to perverse sado-masochistic scenarios is described in Chapter 6.

I believe that Milton also saw a change take place as a result of development, and in the course of the poem we see Adam and Eve change and ultimately face the loss of Eden, mourning this loss and facing their life in the real world. Initially, as we are introduced to the personalities in *Paradise Lost*, we, as readers, are led to sympathise, and to identify with Lucifer, and with Adam and Eve in their reaction to God as unjust and cruel, and we support their rebellion against tyrannical demands. One of the pleasures of the poem, as Fish (1967, 1975) helps us to recognise, is that we are persuaded to reflect and to reconsider this view as we go through a process of relinquishment and loss, something like that which Milton's protagonists go through. We can follow the course taken by Adam and Eve who first rebel and then suffer the consequences of their action eventually to face their shame and guilt and reconcile themselves to a God restored as a symbol of the ideal. However, in order to serve as a symbol the ideal object must be relinquished as a possession so that its loss and the associated loss of omnipotence can be mourned (Segal, 1957).

In contrast to Satan, Adam and Eve are finally reconciled with God and are able to look towards their future as they depart from Paradise. The final departure is both sad and splendid, partly I think because we see the obedience as a submission to reality rather than as a compliance with authority.

They looking back, all th' Eastern side beheld
Of Paradise, so late thir happie seat,

...

Som natural tears they drop'd, but wip'd them soon;
The World was all before them, where to choose
Thir place of rest, and Providence thir guide:
They hand in hand with wandring steps and slow,
Through Eden took thir solitarie way.

(Book Twelve, 649)

Notes

1 This chapter is based in part on Steiner, J. (2013). The Ideal and the Real in Klein and Milton: Some Observations on Reading *Paradise Lost*. *Psychoanalytic Quarterly*, 82, 897–923.
2 Turning to literature has the advantage of a readily available shared area of experience since the examples are either well known or can be easily read up. However, the major disadvantage is that the application of the ideas to specific clinical situations is missing or conjectural. Even so my frame of reference throughout continues to be clinical and I always try to apply what I have learned from poets, dramatists and novelists to the clinical situation. I hope the ideas will be sufficiently interesting to lead the psychoanalytic reader to test them in his clinical practice.
3 Reference to Klein's Lectures in technique are listed as (2017) the year they were published. They were given in 1936 and were later discovered in the Klein Trust Archives.
4 The phrase "to love and to work" does not appear directly in Freud's writings, although it seems to be implied in several places for example when he states, "The communal life of human beings had, therefore, a two-fold foundation: the compulsion to work, which was created by external necessity, and the power of love ... " (Freud, 1930, p. 101).

2 Learning from Milton

The dangerous gap between the real and the ideal[1]

In this chapter I continue to look at what we can learn from *Paradise Lost* and here I pay special attention to the consequences of disillusion where facing the loss of Paradise can enable the development of symbolic function. When we identify with the ideal object and own and possess Paradise the benefits are concrete and real. In the process of disillusionment we come to face reality and mourn the loss of perfection. I suggest that it is in the process of mourning that projections are returned to the self so that a separation between the actual object and its symbol can emerge.

Milton depicts God as a symbol of perfection, especially one that represents perfect goodness, and it is striking to find, as I shall shortly describe, that Klein views the good breast in just the same way. When we contemplate such ideal objects we become aware of the gap between what we are and the perfection they possess and the primitive response is to bridge that gap by engaging in a narcissistic identification with the ideal and to harbour the illusion that we have that perfection for ourselves. Thus we engage in the earliest and most universal of phantasies that creates the narcissistic illusion, "The breast is a part of me, I am the breast". If and when we are able to re-engage with reality a more or less traumatic process of disillusion allows this phantasy to be transformed into one that acknowledges dependence in what Freud called an anaclitic relationship. "I have it" that is "I am not it" (Freud, 1941, p. 299). The working through of the disillusion is of momentous significance not simply because it establishes a more realistic relationship with the object but because it is in the course of relinquishment of the concrete possession of the ideal object that symbolic function is established and the concrete object in the internal world is replaced by a symbol. As mourning is worked through separateness is re-established as elements that belong to the object are returned to the object and those belonging to the self are reclaimed by the self. It is Hanna Segal who suggested that it is this separateness that enables the symbol to be differentiated from the thing symbolised.

This transformation from the concrete to the symbolic is a major developmental step but it is, like all developmental steps, unstable and further regressions towards the concrete are bound to occur. Moreover, as will be

seen as we examine Milton's view of the ideal and compare it with that of
Klein, the concrete continues to exist in the mind of the individual.
I suggest that it functions as a measure or standard of the ideal by which
we judge ourselves but remains a goal to be aspired to rather than one that
can be realised. Indeed phantasies in which we become ideal ourselves are
at the core of narcissistic omnipotence and as in the ancient Greek notion
of *hubris* are described as forbidden by God. This makes sense of the puzzling presence of the Tree of Knowledge in the Garden of Eden, and eating
the fruit can be seen as an act of hubris in which Adam and Eve tried to be
equal to God. This led to the traumatic end of the Garden of Eden Illusion
and brought home the fact that the illusion was only possible in a state of
ignorance. Once we have knowledge of reality we can no longer claim perfection for ourselves. It can however remain as an ideal and serve as
a symbol of perfect goodness.

It is impressive to observe the remarkable amount of common ground
between Milton's view of God as a symbol of an ideal good object and
Klein's view of the good breast playing a similar role. Both use similar
terms despite the very different context and both describe how the ideal
aspects of the object give rise to the painful perception of the gap between
the ordinary limitations of the individual and the perfection of the ideal
which is provocatively present but unattainable. It is the gap between the
human and the divine in Milton's setting and that between the infant and
the ideal breast in Klein's descriptions that is seen to provoke envy and to
stimulate attempts to bridge the gap through phantasies of omnipotent possession of the ideal. Again, both Milton and Klein suggest that if the
omnipotence can be recognised as an illusion, possession of the ideal can be
relinquished and its loss can be experienced and mourned. When this
becomes possible the ideal object comes to be installed as a symbol in the
internal world where it can serve as a measure of goodness, which is aspired
to but not possessed.

I will describe how Milton allows us to see God as a symbol of perfection
but at the same time offers a view of a tyrannical father prohibiting and
punishing transgressions. If he is viewed as a symbol of perfection the
expulsion of Lucifer from Heaven can be seen to be a logical necessity. God
cannot be partly good and partly bad or he ceases to be a measure of perfect goodness. The division between good and bad as represented by
Heaven and Hell then comes to represent the dictates of reality in the symbolic field in which ideal good and ideal bad objects exist and remain separate if they are to remain perfect.

If, on the other hand, God has human attributes the division between
Heaven and Hell can be seen as a defensive use of splitting, creating
a narcissistic superiority to which the child is pressured to submit. I will
suggest that we all start from the latter view and try to rebel against the
authority of the father in order to develop an individual identity and personal moral judgements. The tyrannical father is of course the version

Freud described when he suggested that the resolution of oedipal conflict arose because of the threat of castration, and I have proposed that a rebellious disobedience can be necessary for healthy development (Steiner, 2011).

It is in the aftermath of rebellion that important changes take place provided the loss of the good object can be worked through. The disobedience leading to the oedipal murder liberated Adam and Eve as they gave in to their omnipotent phantasies but because they could accept the difference between the human and the divine they were able to work through their guilt and shame and install the good object as a symbol of goodness to be aspired to. This was not the case with Lucifer who was unable to accept his guilt and remained unrepentant.

Accepting the difference between the human and the divine, between the child and the parents as natural and part of reality rather than imposed by authority leads to a consideration of other differences that also make up elements of reality. In addition to the difference between the generations, we have to accept a difference between male and female with the implication that complementarity is essential to creativity. Possibly most central is the acceptance of the difference between life and death that comes with an acknowledgement of mortality as part of the human condition that distinguishes us from God.

Self-doubt is then a feature of being human because we are always in conflict having the voice of Satan in one ear and the voice of God in the other. It is this struggle that Adam and Eve contended with and it is the consequences of their choice that the poem explores. Such conflict is not something that God is subject to because he has to represent ideal goodness and even Satan, who has moments of doubt in the poem, recognises that if he is to represent absolute evil he cannot really waver. For Man, however, almost every question is open to doubt as we consider if we are a child or an adult, a man or a woman, and especially perhaps if we are mortal or immortal. In each situation we are tempted by Satan to take his side against God and especially against his injunction to relinquish omnipotence and accept who we are. In Chapter 1 I used Money-Kyrle's description of the facts of life to refer to these basic issues that we become aware of as we face reality and differentiate ourselves from the Gods whose possession of omnipotence is not within our reach. Each of these facts involves a difference and each is dependent on the recognition of the passage of time.

Shame of exposure

Milton elaborates the Biblical account of the possession and then loss of Paradise in extraordinary detail and this allows us to make interesting new connections to situations and phantasies that are met in early development and relived in the transference. My initial interest in the poem arose from a concern with feelings of shame and humiliation which appear in a sudden and shocking way after Adam and Eve eat of the Tree of Knowledge and recognise that they are naked. They are expelled from the Garden of Eden and we see the expulsion as familiar and terrible. The evident suffering is suffused with shame as the couple are exposed having mistakenly assumed a narcissistic complacency that turns out to have been an illusion. I have previously described a similar appearance of shame and humiliation when patients emerge from the protection of a psychic retreat (Steiner, 2006, 2011), and I have thought of the expulsion from Eden to closely parallel the feelings of an infant forced out from an idealised place where he felt himself to be the sole possessor of the breast and with it of the mother's love.

Indeed *Paradise Lost* convinces the reader of the remarkable amount of common ground between Milton and contemporary psychoanalysts which allows us to approach the poetic drama just as we might approach clinical material. Despite the apparent disparity between material from the consulting room and that of a poet, and also despite the gap between what seems to be a concrete literal interpretation of events and a modern sceptical view, I was impressed by how little the difference of time and of outlook affects our capacity to appreciate the poem or to see the relevance to psychoanalytic work. Many of the ideas not only prefigure our psychoanalytic understanding but also remind us that these themes have been around for a very long time, and can sometimes be more clearly articulated by poets than by psychoanalysts.

It is clear that neither Milton nor his audience would have formulated the story of such epic events in terms of early infantile experience. Scholars and critics have studied his poetry in relation to his political and personal beliefs, his writing on divorce, his blindness, and the political and religious climate he lived in, better to understand his own view of the world. I have tried to dip into the enormous volume of critical literature on Milton's work (Ricks, 1963, Empson, 1965, Fish, 1967, 1975, Bloom, 1975, Elledge, 1975, Beer, 2008), and have read some of the many papers by psychoanalysts (Zimmerman, 1981, Rudat, 1985, Rudnytsky, 1988, Fulmer, 2006), but I realised that it was beyond me to attempt a review. Instead I decided to concentrate on the effect that the poem had on me as a reader interested in a psychoanalytic understanding of unconscious phantasy.

The ideal as a symbol of perfection

Milton's account helps us to differentiate between the ideal as a concrete belief on the one hand and as a symbol and measure of ideal goodness on the other. It also reveals the close parallel between the views of Milton and Klein both of whom believe that for healthy development an ideal object must initially be installed in the internal world.

I will describe how Adam and Eve are repeatedly warned that they must not aspire to omnipotence and suggest that for Milton obedience was primarily an obedience to the dictates of a reality that emphasises the gap between the human and the divine. Eating of the fruit of the forbidden tree led to an awareness of a number of critical differences, and as well as the difference between the omnipotence of God compared to the limited powers of Man, these include the difference between good and evil, between life and death, and even between male and female. Had they not rebelled Adam and Eve would have remained ignorant and hence trapped in the illusion that omnipotent possession of the ideal was desirable and even possible.

It is interesting that Milton considered that envy played a major part to incite disobedience in both Lucifer and Adam and Eve. He recognised that they were sorely provoked by the way they were exposed to feelings of envy and jealousy when perfection was paraded before them and withheld from them. Both rebelled and both faced a humiliating defeat but a critical difference between them became apparent in the way they dealt with their humiliation. Adam and Eve eventually accept their shame and guilt and are reconciled to God while Lucifer remains defiant and dedicated to evil. The pain of shame and humiliation is also vividly described by Milton who connects it to the terrible change of status connected with the fall and the loss of God's love. Having believed they were special and superior both Satan and Adam and Eve fall to inferior and contemptible positions which make them vulnerable to terrible punishments.

The role of the ideal object as a measure of goodness for Milton and for Klein

If the narcissistic possession of the ideal can be relinquished and recognised to have been an illusion, the ideal object can be relinquished and mourned and in the process installed in the internal world as a symbol. For Milton God is real but also functions as a symbol of ideal goodness and 300 years later Klein offers a view of the ideal that seems to me to be remarkably similar to his. She too saw the ideal object as real, and also serving as a model or ideal of goodness.

> We find in the analysis of our patients that the breast in its good aspect is the prototype of maternal goodness, inexhaustible patience and generosity, as well as of creativeness. It is these phantasies and instinctual needs that so enrich the primal object that it remains the foundation for hope, trust and belief in goodness.
>
> (Klein, 1957, p. 180)

For both Milton and Klein the good object serves precisely the same function as a foundation for hope, trust and belief in goodness, and both are aware that this perfection presents difficulties. In particular a gap is seen to exist between the perfect ideal object and our ordinary human abilities and achievements. It is this gap that gave Satan his opportunity because he knew that when the gap becomes unbearable it is likely to be bridged by phantasies of omnipotence.

Milton believed in a God who existed as a real external presence, and whose perfection provoked envy and led to wishes on the part of Lucifer and Adam and Eve to equal him. Similarly for Klein the ideal object is, in the mind of the infant, a real external presence, and the infant internalises this ideal object and uses it as a measure of the ideal. He may also form a concrete narcissistic identification with this ideal object, "I am the breast".[2]

Klein considered further that, later in development, as the possession of the ideal is gradually relinquished and mourned, the concrete is transformed into a symbol and becomes something like Freud's ego-ideal (Segal, 1957). Indeed we could consider the process to involve a movement from a narcissistic ideal-ego to a symbolic ego-ideal. Nevertheless the concrete image of an actual good object, that actually did exist, remains as a deeply held belief and is probably never completely relinquished. Moreover even though it is clearly based on splitting, idealisation and illusion it serves an important function as a model that inspires us and alongside which we can be judged.

I believe that Milton also saw a change taking place in Adam and Eve which enables them ultimately to face the loss of Eden, to mourn this loss and to accept their life in the real world. Initially, as we are intro-duced to the personalities in *Paradise Lost*, we readers, are led to sympa-thise, and to identify with Lucifer, and with Adam and Eve in their reaction to God as unjust and cruel, and we support their rebellion against tyrannical demands. One of the pleasures of the poem, as Fish (1967, 1975) helps us to recognise, is that we are persuaded to reflect and to reconsider this view as we go through a process of relinquishment and loss, something like that which Milton's protagonists go through. We can follow the course taken by Adam and Eve who first rebel and then suffer the consequences of their action eventually to face their shame and guilt and reconcile themselves to a God restored as a symbol of the ideal. However, in order to serve as a symbol the ideal object must be relin-quished as a possession so that its loss and the associated loss of omnipo-tence can be mourned (Segal, 1957).

The gap between the human and the divine

In *Paradise Lost*, Man eventually accepts the difference between himself and God, through painful struggles with the loss of the ideal as a possession. We see him bowing to fate, mourning the loss of Paradise, and accepting the loss of omnipotence. God's goodness and power can then become a symbol and measure of goodness rather than an achievable state. We have contrasted this acceptance with the recalcitrance of Satan who never relinquishes his struggle to equal God or, when this failed as it inevitably must, at least to injure him by attacking Man whom he views as God's most important creation.

Milton tackles the problem of Man's insatiable demand for perfection by making a distinction between the human and the divine. For him God is perfect and omnipotent in contradistinction to Man who can only enjoy the pleasures of Paradise if he submits to the conditions demanded by God. Obedience is the price of Paradise and the injunction not to eat of the Tree of Knowledge emphasises the limitations that Man has to accept. Man's good fortune is dependent on the goodwill of God and the omnipotence of God cannot be emulated.

The perennial dangers of omnipotence and hubris

Throughout the poem Milton is concerned with the dangers that arise when Man is tempted to assume omnipotence for himself. Warnings of this danger are repeatedly given to Adam and Eve in *Paradise Lost* and this temptation for Man to become or to make himself equal to a God is a concern that is found in most cultures often represented as a human challenge to the status of God. This eating from the Tree of Knowledge gains its significance as a challenge to the authority and omnipotence of God.

It is an example, I believe, of the universal danger of hubris in which man aspires to equal or defeat the Gods. In Greek mythology it was expressed at the Temple of Apollo at Delphi by the two injunctions, *gnōthi seautón* (know thyself) and *mēdén ágan* (nothing in excess) both of which must be obeyed in order to avoid hubris and claim more than is one's due. One interpretation of the injunction not to eat of the Tree of Knowledge is similar. Know thyself as human and hence accept your limitations and do not seek the excess of omnipotence.

There are many myths that describe the disaster that results when humans challenge the superiority of Gods. In one instance, Phaeton failed to control the horses that his father Helios uses to draw the sun across the sky, and not only killed himself but set much of the earth on fire. In another myth Niobe Queen of Thebes boasted of her 14 children to the Goddess Leto whose two children Apollo and Artemis were sired by Zeus. Her hubris was punished in a simple and brutal way when all of her children were hunted down and killed. The story of Icarus is perhaps the best-known warning not to over-look human limitations. Excited by the wings that his father Daedalus designed he attached them with wax and then flew too near the sun.

The humanising of god by depicting him as an authoritarian father

The God described in *Paradise Lost* is one of perfect goodness and justice, but at one and the same time, is shown behaving like an authoritarian father. He is presented as powerful, despotic, unforgiving, cruel and provocative, demanding obedience and provoking hatred and rebellion. Milton allows us to see that God is often experienced as far from ideal, and that when he is viewed as a person his tyranny provokes rebellion.

In the same way our patients imbue their objects, for example their actual parents and their actual analysts, with ideal qualities and when they fail to live up to the expectations they are often experienced as persecutors. Milton helps us to recognise that the idealised and powerful good object that provokes envy may also be seen as unjustly exercising power to exploit the patient. I suggest that in all these situations it may be difficult or impossible to differentiate envy of good objects from rebellion against bad ones.

Rebellion and disobedience, when successful, simultaneously attack good objects alongside the bad, and it is only after the fact, with the realisation of this destruction, that love can be liberated and feelings of guilt and remorse can usher in the depressive position. The hatred of the real object is then a compound of envious attacks on its goodness and a rebellion against its badness. Frequently, it is only after the attacks have been carried out that the goodness can be recognised and only then that love and the wish for reparation can be liberated. Here we can see the difference between Milton's portrayals of Man and of Satan. When their disobedience is discovered both suffer the painful humiliation of being exposed as defiantly omnipotent, but Man becomes humble and contrite, his heart softened and his love released, while Satan retreats to an unrepentant devotion to evil and destructiveness.

An important step in the acceptance of reality is taken when a distinction is made between God as a symbol of the ideal and God as a severe and punitive figure who both judges and punishes. I have argued that this distinction is what Milton used to "Justify the ways of God to Men" and that it involves "emancipating the ego" (Britton, 2003) by taking back the judging function from the super-ego into the ego.

If we allow Satan to persuade us that God is a tantalising cruel father, placing the forbidden fruit in full view of Adam and Eve and then punishing them for disobeying him we forget that it is reality that determines a limit to omnipotence. We prefer to believe that God has ceased to be a measure of perfection and instead is behaving like a tyrannical father. If that were to have been the case it would have been right to rebel against the prohibitions perhaps especially those against knowledge and curiosity but if the rebellion is against the limitations imposed by reality the ultimate need is to submit. Freud himself described the relinquishment of oedipal phantasies as resulting from the castration threats of the father rather than from a consideration of the reality of the child's capacities and I argue that the acceptance of this kind of authority leads to resentment and revenge. However it is frequently difficult to judge if it is reality or authority that demands submission and it is not unusual in analysis to find that the judgement is evaded by submission to the analyst experienced as an authoritarian father who tells the patient what he should do. Eventually, however, if he is to accept his independent position the child, and after him the Man, has to make these judgements himself and this enables God to be reinstated as an ideal which can serve as an inspiration and a model by which he can measure himself.

Milton shows how easy it was for Adam and Eve to be seduced by Satan into believing that God was a jealous tyrant against whom it was right to rebel. Omnipotence is inevitably a temptation when the gap between what is allowed to humans and what they observe in the Gods, becomes too great. Freud recognised that the father inevitably stimulates identification,

> "You ought to be like this (like your father)". [But that] "It also comprises the prohibition: You may not be like this (like your father)—that is, you may not do all that he does; some things are his prerogative".
>
> (Freud, 1923, p. 34)

This distinction is caught in the Latin phrase "*Quod licet Jovi non licet Bovi*", often translated as "Gods may do what cattle may not". It indicates the existence of a double standard which emphasises the high status of Jove and the lowly one of the child.

What we recognise today is that to successfully engage in a creative development a rebellion against the father is necessary and that in the unconscious this amounts to his overthrow and murder. I have always felt it is to Eve's great credit that she was able to lead the rebellion and of course eventually to pay the price when reality was re-established. It is also to Adam's credit that he chose to remain loyal to her and face reality with her by leaving Eden.

When the gap between the human and the divine becomes too great it is lessened in two ways. Man elevates himself through omnipotence and at the same time he diminishes God by attributing human qualities to him. Satan uses the attractions of omnipotence to persuade Eve that she can rebel and assume omnipotence for herself but in his seduction he attributes human qualities to God by describing him as tyrannical and even suggests that he is capable of feeling envy.

The ideal-ego and the ego-ideal

Freud himself tackled a distinction between the concrete and the symbolic in his early descriptions of the ideal-ego and the ego-ideal. In his discussion of narcissism (Freud, 1914) he writes, "We can say that ... man has set up an *ideal* in himself by which he measures his actual ego ..." (p. 93). This is the *ego ideal*. By contrast, the *ideal ego* results from the subject's narcissism leading to an illusion in which, "the infantile ego, finds itself possessed of *every perfection*" (p. 93).

The ego-ideal is an aspiration and a measure of excellence by which the ego can be judged while the ideal-ego is an illusion that the state of excellence has actually been achieved. Later Freud (1923) used the terms interchangeably and subsumed them both into the super-ego, and Hanly (1984) points out that this obscures the important difference between the two terms. He describes the ego-ideal as, "a state of becoming", whereas, "The ideal-ego is a self-image that is distorted by idealization but it may be experienced as more real than the ego itself" (p. 253). Loewald (1962) had earlier put forward a similar view suggesting that the ideal-ego represents a recapturing of the original primary-narcissistic perfection of the child by a primitive identification with omnipotent parental figures. Britton (2003) agrees and suggests that the ideal-ego arises by identification of the self with the ego-ideal. He sees it as a deviation from normal development and based on a narcissistic identification. Essentially these authors differentiate the ego-ideal as a symbol or model of perfection from the narcissistically grandiose assumption of the ideal-ego which is based on an already achieved perfection through identification.

Britton (2003) also points out that Freud not only dropped the distinction between the ideal-ego and the ego-ideal but that, in his picture of the super-ego, he included both the ideal as a measure of goodness and the critical agency that judges it. He suggests that if healthy development is to proceed, the judgemental function has to be wrested from the super-ego by the ego. In his view the ego can use the ideal as a standard by which it is judged but that the judging process has to be recognised as an ego function. In this way the ego is emancipated from the earlier dominance of the super-ego. These distinctions are very relevant to the relationship of Man with God in which it is God who both sets the standard of goodness and judges and punishes Man if he fails to meet the standard. It is possible to rebel against the authority of God and to take onto ourselves the capacity to make judgements while retaining the idea of God as a measure of perfection alongside which we can compare ourselves.

Of course these ideals can become concretised and some of the most terrible wars are fought on the grounds that one God or one political system is superior to another. Some of the differences between Gods that are seen to be so critical turn out to be impressively minor, and I think are sustained through the narcissism of minor differences (Gabbard, 1993). In a similar manner the devout belief in God that Milton entertained and the more sceptical version of contemporary attitudes are often seen as very different and yet seem to me to be quite similar. What is much more significant is our attitude to our belief in our Gods or Political ideals which can involve treating them as symbols of an unattainable excellence or alternately viewing them as goals already achieved and needing to be defended. Later in Chapter 8 I discuss the importance of irony which can help us to temper our passionate beliefs with self-doubt as we manage both to believe and not to believe in our ideals. It is such self-doubt that is beyond the means of Satan as he attempts to replace a belief in goodness with one of envy and hatred.

Satan's guile

When Satan discovered that God had placed the Tree of Knowledge within their grasp and then forbade Adam and Eve to touch it he saw how provocative this would be. This is important in understanding why they rebelled.

> Say first, for Heav'n hides nothing from thy view
> Nor the deep Tract of Hell, say first what cause
> Mov'd our Grand Parents in that happy State,
> Favour'd of Heav'n so highly, to fall off
> From thir Creator, and transgress his Will
> For one restraint, Lords of the World besides?
> Who first seduc'd them to that foul revolt?
> Th' infernal Serpent; he it was, whose guile
> Stird up with Envy and Revenge, deceiv'd
> The Mother of Mankind ...
>
> (Book One, 36)

Adam and Eve were created, "Lords of the World", but for that "one restraint", and it was that restraint which became their downfall. Satan was quick to find this weak point in God's plan and leapt to capitalise on it by presenting God as cruel, tormenting Man by putting something so desirable within his reach and then forbidding access to it. Satan speaks as follows:

> ... all is not theirs it seems:
> One fatal Tree there stands of Knowledge call'd, Forbidden them to taste:
>   Knowledge forbidd'n?
> Suspicious, reasonless. Why should thir Lord
> Envie them that? can it be sin to know,
> Can it be death? and do they onely stand
> By Ignorance, is that thir happie state,
> The proof of thir obedience and thir faith?
> O fair foundation laid whereon to build
> Thir ruine! Hence I will excite thir minds
> With more desire to know, and to reject
> Envious commands, invented with designe
> To keep them low whom knowledge might exalt ...
>
> (Book Four, 525)

Satan uses this argument in his seduction of Eve, even humanising God to the point that he suggested that he was capable of feeling envy. In this way he was able to seduce Eve to believe that God was not really very different from herself.

> *What can your knowledge hurt him, or this Tree*
> *Impart against his will if all be his?*

Or is it envie, and can envie dwell
In Heav'nly brests? these, these and many more
Causes import your need of this fair Fruit.
Goddess humane, reach then, and freely taste.
(Book Four, 730)

Of course we know that it is Satan speaking and it is *his* claim that God is susceptible to human feelings which is to deny the divinity and perfection of God. Satan himself is consumed with envy and has just come from spying on Adam and Eve, sensually "imparadised" in one another's arms. It was the mutual adoration and Eve's delight in her submission that was too much for Satan to bear:

aside the Devil turnd
For envie, yet with jealous leer maligne
Ey'd them askance, and to himself thus plaind.
Sight hateful, sight tormenting! thus these two
    Imparadis't in one anothers arms
The happier Eden, shall enjoy thir fill
Of bliss on bliss, while I to Hell am thrust,
Where neither joy nor love, but fierce desire,
Among our other torments not the least,
Still unfulfill'd with pain of longing pines.
(Book Four, 510)

Satan feels himself to be excluded from the bliss of the primal couple and describes his Hell as a place where he continues to feel tormented by an intense desire. Despite our awareness that Satan is driven by envy, we feel compassion for the pain he feels as he witnesses Adam and Eve "imparadised" in each other's arms. This is even more understandable when we hear the history of his relationship with God and of the rebellion that led to his expulsion from Heaven.

Milton's sympathetic understanding of the disobedience of Lucifer

Before his fall Satan was known as Lucifer and enjoyed the status as God's leading Archangel and favourite. He had enjoyed an idealised relationship with God and had no rivals until suddenly and without warning the arrival of Christ displaced him and led to a brutal disillusionment. Milton recognises the enormity of this provocation and views his grievance sympathetically.

Hear all ye Angels, Progenie of Light,
Thrones, Dominations, Princedoms, Vertues, Powers,
Hear my Decree, which unrevok't shall stand.
This day I have begot whom I declare
My onely Son, and on this holy Hill

Him have anointed, whom ye now behold
At my right hand; your Head I him appoint;
And by my Self have sworn to him shall bow
All knees in Heav'n, and shall confess him Lord: ...
(Book Five, 608)

Once again, in sympathy with Lucifer's grievance the reader reacts to the injustice and insensitivity of God's announcement by attributing human qualities to God. We see him as a cruel tyrant and view Satan's rebellion as justified. Milton leads us to take this view and then persuades us that it is mistaken. It was envy of God and jealousy of his newly begotten son that provoked Lucifer to disobey and it was envy that prevented him from accepting God's right to enjoy his relationship with his newly begotten son.

Satan, so call him now, his former name
Is heard no more in Heav'n; he of the first,
If not the first Arch-Angel, great in Power,
In favour and præeminence, yet fraught
With envie against the Son of God, that day
Honourd by his great Father, and proclaimd
Messiah King anointed, could not beare
Through pride that sight, & thought himself impaird. (Book Five, 665)

He thinks himself impaired, that is reduced by the raising of another, and taking his supporters with him he incites them to rebellion, anticipating that, like him, they will find that it was difficult enough to pay homage to God alone and to do so to his son as well was just too much.

Knee-tribute yet unpaid, prostration vile,
Too much to one, but double how endur'd,
To one and to his image now proclaim'd?
But what if better counsels might erect
Our minds and teach us to cast off this Yoke?
Will ye submit your necks, and chuse to bend
The supple knee? ye will not, if I trust
To know ye right, or if ye know your selves.
(Book Five, 785)

In Satan's eyes God had become a domineering father who had no understanding of the child's reaction to the parents' adoration of his new-born sibling. It is this provocation that led to the terrible war in Heaven in which Lucifer was able to enlist an army of angels, as many as a "third part of Heav'ns Host", in his attempt to overthrow a God who was seen as unjust. But later we recognise that if God is perfect he cannot be unjust, and we shift to the view that Lucifer is driven by envy and narcissistic pride because he cannot tolerate seeing himself diminished.

Here we also get a taste of God's severity and ruthlessness.

> Him the Almighty Power
> Hurld headlong flaming from th' Ethereal Skie
> With hideous ruine and combustion down
> To bottomless perdition, there to dwell
> In Adamantine Chains and penal Fire,
> Who durst defie th' Omnipotent to Arm.
>
> (Book One, 49)

Lucifer's fall evokes the image of an infant who is abruptly confronted with the reality of a third object in the oedipal triangle. A new baby is announced and the infant feels displaced from his unique place in which he lived in the illusion that the breast was his possession. He feels displaced from a Paradise, in which he can merge with the ideal object, "I'm the breast and the breast is me", to a position of separateness in which he feels that, "I need the breast, which is not me". This often seems to lead to a realisation that "it is not uniquely mine either", which may be equated with the conviction that "I am not loved at all" (Sodre, 2008, 2012).

Lucifer was dethroned from the belief that his place in Heaven was second only to God in the Great Chain of Being (Bunnin and Yu, 2004). He had believed himself to be, *"First Arch-Angel, great in Power/In favour and præeminence"*, and he could not accommodate to the new situation. When he realised that God's love was not uniquely his he was deeply humiliated and when he could not be persuaded that he was still loved, he could not relent and was hurled headlong into chaos. Ultimately when he recovered from the shock his reaction was to create a psychotic organisation out of his corner of chaos and to reverse the humiliation by trying to defeat God in a struggle over power (Segal, 2007).

Having been expelled from his position as the imagined favourite the infant has to accept his new position in the family and this involves an understanding of his place in the hierarchical family structure. Milton helps us to understand the importance of hierarchy and how difficult it is to accept a lower place in the pecking order.

Structure, hierarchy, and envy

In order to instruct Man and to impart what knowledge he is allowed to have God sends the kindly angel Raphael to answer Adam's questions. These questions are evidence of Adam and Eve's curiosity and search for knowledge and although Raphael does provide some information he repeatedly reminds Adam that there are limits to what he is allowed to know, and specifically that the fruit of the Tree of Knowledge is forbidden. Raphael emphasises the importance of order, structure and hierarchy, in which man has to learn to know his place, in particular that he is different from God.

Moreover, the difference between Man and God is the chief of many differences that are encountered in relation to others, and many of these differences cause such pain that it is difficult for us to see them as aspects of reality rather than as injustices inflicted on us. Money-Kyrle (1968, 1971) has singled out three facts that are so fundamental that he refers to them as the "Facts of Life". He describes these facts as, "The recognition of the breast as a supremely good object, the recognition of the parents' intercourse as a supremely creative act, and the recognition of the inevitability of time and ultimately death".

These three facts all have to do with the recognition of differences, particularly those that we confront in the Oedipus situation in which the child attributes ideal qualities to the relationship between the parents from which he feels excluded. He cannot accept that there is a difference between the generations and, in denial of his smallness, he attempts omnipotently to enter the primal scene by identification with one or other parent. He also comes up against the fact that differences in gender give rise to inequalities in the procreative couple and eventually he is forced to recognise the reality of the passage of time. We come up against this last fact of life, the passage of time, not only by the facts of ageing and death, but before that, by the repeated experience that all good things come to an end, and hence even the good object cannot be enjoyed forever. These facts give meaning and structure to the child's early view of the world, but they are difficult to tolerate and to varying degrees are denied and distorted by the developing child.

The difficulty of tolerating them is prominent in Paradise Lost especially in the many hierarchies that emphasise difference and rank, and that can easily lead to issues of superiority and inferiority. In Paradise, Man is superior to animals, each in their natural order, and even in Heaven there are clear distinctions. Milton frequently shows angels assembled and ordered with military precision in their various ranks.

> Under thir Hierarchs in orders bright
> Ten thousand thousand Ensignes high advanc'd,
> Standards and Gonfalons twixt Van and Reare
> Streame in the Aire, and for distinction serve
> Of Hierarchies, of Orders, and Degrees.[3]
>
> (Book Five, 590)

It is when this structure is disturbed that dissension breaks out in Heaven and later in Paradise. If a familiar hierarchy is disrupted then the individual steps out, or feels pushed out, of his allotted place and easily becomes either superior and triumphant, or looked down on and humiliated. If our place in the hierarchy is a function of reality it may eventually have to be faced even though it provokes envy and jealousy of those with greater advantages. However, hierarchy can also be used to "put people in their place", to inflict humiliation on them, and to exercise power over them. This is often how patients in analysis see it and it is precisely how Lucifer saw it, since for him obedience meant a subservient submission to a greater power, which left behind a sense of injustice and resentment.

Creativity and difference

Recognising the parents' intercourse as a supremely creative act emphasises the oedipal triangle and the primal scene as the arena of creativity. This too provokes envy of the primal couple so amply illustrated in Satan's torment when he witnesses Adam and Eve "imparadised". It involves a further recognition that creative relationships, for example between man and woman on the one hand, and between mother and baby on the other, involve a recognition of difference and are very provocative of envy. Indeed Klein believed that creativity is the quality that is often deeply envied and hated.

Raphael's description of the creation of the world emphasises the imposition of structure upon chaos. At the same time it is replete with metaphors of pregnancy, fecundity, and sexuality.

> He took the golden Compasses, prepar'd
> In Gods Eternal store, to circumscribe
> This Universe, and all created things:
> One foot he center'd, and the other turn'd
> Round through the vast profunditie obscure,
> And said, thus farr extend, thus farr thy bounds,
> This be thy just Circumference, O World.
> Thus God the Heav'n created, thus the Earth,
> Matter unform'd and void: Darkness profound
> Cover'd th' Abyss: but on the watrie calme
> His brooding wings the Spirit of God outspred,
> And vital vertue infus'd, and vital warmth
> Throughout the fluid Mass, but downward purg'd
> The black tartareous cold Infernal dregs
> Adverse to life: then founded, then conglob'd
> Like things to like, the rest to several place
> Disparted, and between spun out the Air,
> And Earth self ballanc't on her Center hung.
>   (Book Seven, 242)

The world is created by dividing and assembling (conglobing), vital virtue and vital warmth, is infused, and the anti-life forces are downward purged. The act of creation circumscribes an area of chaos and transforms it by giving it structure. There are resonances with the mother's love that can rescue a lost child from chaos and also of childbirth under God's brooding wings. It is precisely this creativity, and the structure and meaning that results from it, that is so impressive and admirable that it is also a potent stimulus to envy. The goal of the envious attack so precisely portrayed by Satan, is to eliminate difference and to recreate chaos, where there is no structure or meaning and nothing to provoke envy (Klein, 1957, Money-Kyrle, 1968).

It is instructive to compare the fate of Adam and Eve with that of Satan as each of them are obliged to face their new situation after their disobedience and fall. Hanna Segal pointed out (Segal, 2007), that each of them succumbed to the temptations of omnipotence and that even though their situation has much in common the outcome and their reaction to it is very different.

Repentance and compassion

Having expelled Adam and Eve from Eden, God, in the person of Christ, is moved to compassion by their contrition and provides comfort and understanding by covering their nakedness with clothing.

> Then pittying how they stood
> Before him naked to the aire, that now
> Must suffer change, disdain'd not to begin
> Thenceforth the form of servant to assume,
> As when he wash'd his servants feet so now
> As Father of his Familie he clad
> Thir nakedness with Skins of Beasts, or slain,
> Nor hee thir outward only with the Skins
> Of Beasts, but inward nakedness, much more
> Opprobrious, with his Robe of righteousness ...
> (Book Ten, 220)

Both Adam and Eve, having displeased God, next go through the various feelings that are familiar to the person facing loss. They are angry, guilty, and ashamed, and face their despair sometimes with resentment but ultimately with acceptance. Eventually Adam encourages Eve to bear their punishment and tries to persuade her that it will have its compensations.

> Pains only in Child-bearing were foretold,
> And bringing forth, soon recompenc't with joy,
> Fruit of thy Womb: On mee the Curse aslope
> Glanc'd on the ground, with labour I must earne
> My bread; what harm? Idleness had bin worse;
> My labour will sustain me; and least Cold
> Or Heat should injure us, his timely care
> Hath unbesaught provided, and his hands
> Cloath'd us unworthie, pitying while he judg'd ...
> (Book Ten, 1059)

God will ease their suffering and then when their time has come they can prepare for death.

> What better can we do, then to the place
> Repairing where he judg'd us, prostrate fall
> Before him reverent, and there confess
> Humbly our faults, and pardon beg, with tears
> Watering the ground, and with our sighs the Air [Book Ten, 1090]
> Thus they in lowliest plight repentant stood
> Praying, for from the Mercie-seat above
> Prevenient Grace descending had remov'd
> The stonie from thir hearts, & made new flesh
> Regenerate grow instead, that sighs now breath'd Unutterable, which the
>   Spirit of prayer
> Inspir'd, and wing'd for Heav'n with speedier flight
> Then loudest Oratorie.

> (Book Eleven, 8)

In a marked contrast to Adam and Eve, Satan remains unrepentant and his dedication to revenge is typical of reactions to the disappointment associated with disillusion. This reaction is discussed in more detail in Chapter 6 where the perverse defences against disillusion are presented. Here we can note that despite his assertion that it is "*Better to reign in Hell, then serve in Heav'n*" *[Book One, 263]*, and his presentation as the epitome of absolute evil, Milton allows him some more human characteristics and he even wavers, considering the possibility that he too could repent and make his peace with God.

> Is there no place
> Left for Repentance, none for Pardon left?
> None left but by submission; and that word
> Disdain forbids me ...

In sadness however his realises that there is no way back and it is this that leads him to espouse evil as his goal.

> So farewel Hope, and with Hope farewel Fear,
> Farewel Remorse: all Good to me is lost;
> Evil be thou my Good ... (Book One, 110)

Adam and eve face their future

Another archangel, Michael, is sent to explain Adam's future and that of his descendants by giving accounts of Biblical events such as the building of

the Tower of Babel, and the Flood. In these accounts Michael warns Adam
that, in contrast to Paradise, the world is both good and bad.

> To shew thee what shall come in future dayes
> To thee and to thy Ofspring; good with bad
> Expect to hear, supernal Grace contending
> With sinfulness of Men; thereby to learn ...

Adam responds to what he has been shown with further protestations of
submission and obedience.

> Greatly instructed I shall hence depart.
> Greatly in peace of thought, and have my fill
> Of knowledge, what this Vessel can containe;
> Beyond which was my folly to aspire.
> Henceforth I learne, that to obey is best,
> And love with feare the onely God ...
> (Book Twelve, 562)

Michael is pleased and sees this subservience as true wisdom. Eve assures
Adam that she is willing to accompany him out of Eden, and they both
agree to submit to God's will.

To "justify the ways of god to men"

It seems to me that Milton wanted to correct a commonly held view that
God resembled an authoritarian figure who imposed his arbitrary will on
the world. To "justify the ways of God to Men" he had to show that it was
a fatal error to attribute human functions to God and in this way to deny
his divinity and hence fail to recognise that his perfection enables him to
function as a symbol and measure of goodness. In this task Milton asks for
guidance from his muse:

> What in me is dark
> Illumin, what is low raise and support;
> That to the highth of this great Argument
> I may assert Eternal Providence,
> And justifie the wayes of God to men.
> (Book 1. 25)

If we allow Satan to persuade us that God is a tantalising cruel father, placing the forbidden fruit in full view of Adam and Eve and then punishing
them for disobeying him we forget that it is reality that determines a limit
to omnipotence. We prefer to believe that God has ceased to be a measure
of perfection and instead is behaving like a tyrannical father. If that were to

have been the case it would have been right to rebel against the prohibitions perhaps especially those against knowledge and curiosity but if the rebellion is against the limitations imposed by reality the ultimate need is to submit.

Eventually however if he is to accept his independent position the child, and after him the Man, has to make these judgements himself and this enables God to be reinstated as an ideal which can serve as an inspiration and a model by which he can measure himself.

Notes

1 Based on Steiner, J. (2013). The Ideal and the Real in Klein and Milton: Some Observations on Reading *Paradise Lost*. *Psychoanalytic Quarterly*, 82, 897–923.
2 Some analysts consider that the ideal is something we are born with, that it exists, hard-wired, in the infant's internal world as a primitive prototype, and that it is this prototype that is projected onto external objects that are then viewed as ideal. Money-Kyrle (1971) linked such prototypes with Bion's ideas of innate pre-conceptions (1962) and also with Plato's theory of ideas. Plato he suggests, considered that, "a particular object is recognized as an imperfect copy of an ideal or general object laid up in heaven", and remarked that, "if, by heaven, we mean our own phylogenetic inheritance ... Plato was here very near the mark".
3 Milton seems mostly to adhere to the classically defined Nine orders of Angels. In descending order of status: Seraphim, Cherubim, Thrones, Dominions, Virtues, Powers, Principalities, Archangels, and Angels (Wikipedia, 2009).

3 The brutality of truth and the importance of kindness[1]

We have seen how the expulsion from Eden was felt to be a terrible cruelty certainly as experienced by Adam and Eve and even more so perhaps as experienced by Satan when he was ejected from Heaven. When our patients express similar views it is important for the analyst to be able to empathise with them and to understand their subjective experience. We do this by imaginatively entering the scenario they are describing and as we put ourselves in their shoes we make a hypothesis of what they might be feeling. At the same time we try to maintain an objective view, partly to test the hypothesis and partly in order to gather information and evaluate the situation from the outside. While subjectively it seems as if a terribly cruel injustice has been done, it frequently becomes apparent that the chief effect of the disillusion was to introduce a return to reality and to expose the idealisation as an illusion. On other occasions it does seem as if an injury has been inflicted and the trauma is not just subjective but corroborated as objectively real.

This means that the dual identities of participant and observer are required if the analyst is to encompass the total situation. He has to be able to identify with his patients and hence to participate in their dramas, but at the same time he has to be able to limit his participation and to be able to withdraw from the identification in order to function as an observer. Later I will discuss the role played by irony in enabling such contradictory attitudes to be reconciled.

In thinking about the effect of a theatrical performance on an audience, I was struck by parallels between the role of the analyst when listening to his patient and that of the spectator of a classical drama. In Aristotle's classical theory of catharsis the emotions of terror and pity are central to the experience of tragedy (Freud, 1906, Turri, 2015). In this situation terror involves a fear of something happening to ourselves while pity, by contrast, is based on feelings for the person whom we are observing. I take this to mean that in the audience we feel terror when we have identified with the hero of the drama and are feeling what we imagine he is feeling. However, we feel pity when we have withdrawn from this identification and are observing the suffering as it is happening, not to us, but to someone we have come to care about.[2]

In the present chapter the fate of the characters in Ibsen's The Wild Duck is considered because it is a vivid example of the cruelty of truth and illustrates how important it is to introduce the facts of life in a humane and kind way. This is clearly of central importance in analysis where the patient cannot be helped to face reality if it is introduced without sensitivity to the way it is experienced. The analyst has to understand how the trauma can seem to be abrupt and unfair even if it is part of ordinary life. As I consider the play I will try both to identify with the characters to understand what they are feeling and also stay separate and consider the situation as a whole.

Ibsen's "The Wild Duck" deals with the growing impact of reality on the lives of protagonists who have been living under the spell of an illusion. It is the sudden dramatic impact of reality as it shatters illusions that gives rise to the play's tragic element. Examining this theme can remind us that illusions serve important functions, and that there are dangers if reality is forced onto an individual who is not equipped to deal with it. We see a protagonist who is determined to expose the truth which turns out to be unbearable and leads to tragic consequences.

The brutality of truth in *The Wild Duck*

The drama in *The Wild Duck* (Ibsen, 1884) centres on a confrontation between truth and illusion that follows the reunion of two childhood friends, Hialmar Ekdal and Gregers Werle. They knew each other when their fathers were business partners prior to the disaster that struck Hialmar's father, Old Ekdal. He was convicted of a fraudulent forestry deal, imprisoned and stripped of his army rank, while Gregers's father, Hakon Werle, was acquitted and went on to become a prosperous merchant.

The humiliated, lowly status of the Ekdal family compared to that of the Werles is evident when the play opens with a sumptuous dinner given by Hakon Werle for his son, who has accepted his father's invitation to return after some 17 years of resentful absence following the death of his mother. In defiance of his father, Gregers invites his friend Hialmar to this dinner, in the course of which Hialmar gives an account of his recovery after his family's disgrace. Thanks to Gregers's father, Hakon, Hialmar has been able to establish a photographic studio and to meet the woman to whom he is now happily married. He adds that his wife, Gina, was once in service with the Werles, and Gregers is shocked when he realises that she was the person who not only kept house for them during the last year of his mother's illness, but also the one with whom his father had a relationship.

Hialmar's presence is an embarrassment to the gathering, and the awkwardness is even more painful when the shabby, doddering Old Ekdal walks through the company and is looked down on by everyone—even by his own son, who averts his gaze.

Hialmar leaves early, and Gregers Werle then confronts his father and attacks him for allowing Old Ekdal to take the blame for the crime that both partners were guilty of. This Hakon Werle denies, and Gregers goes on to accuse him of helping the Ekdals with money to cover up his guilt. Moreover, he also accuses him of covering up his relationship with Gina by marrying her off to Hialmar. Hakon Werle asks if it was Hialmar who has accused him of this, and Gregers tells him that it was his mother who told him about his liaison with Gina. Exasperated, Hakon responds by saying that Gregers sees everything through his mother's eyes and has ignored the alcoholism which clouded her vision. Despite the long-standing animosity between father and son, Hakon is seeking a reconciliation with Gregers and has invited him to return home to join the business as a partner, so that Hakon himself can retire to the country and marry his present housekeeper.

Gregers sees this as an attempt to get him to collude with yet another cover-up by condoning his father's behaviour and concealing the family's ugly secrets, including rumours about his mistreatment of Gregers's mother. As the two argue, Gregers's idealisation of his mother and his hatred of his father clearly emerge, and their row ends with Gregers refusing to support his father. On leaving, he insists that they will never meet again. When his father asks him what he will do if he will not join the business, Gregers proclaims that he has now found his mission in life. It is clear that this mission is to expose the lies of Hialmar's marriage, and we realise this has more to do with exposing his father than with helping his friend.

The remainder of the play takes place in Hialmar's studio, where we see the various illusions and self-deceptions that the Ekdal family live by. Despite these, Hialmar and Gina manage to live a contented life and, albeit with hardships and tensions, they care for each other, so that Hialmar can say, "Our roof may be poor and humble, Gina; but it is home. And with all my heart I say: here dwells my happiness" (Ibsen, 1884, p. 35). They gain great comfort from their love for their daughter, Hedvig, now aged 14, who is described as their greatest joy, but also as their deepest sorrow because she is going blind.

Hialmar Ekdal and Gina cope with their humiliatingly lowered status through enacting a pretence. Hialmar's father Old Ekdal escapes to the attic, which contains a make-believe forest where rabbits and hens are kept, and where he can put on his old uniform and pretend he is still an officer shooting bears. Hialmar, instead of working in his studio, dreams of his great invention, which will restore the family name and allow him to rehabilitate his father. Gina supports these illusions, keeps the business going, economises to make ends meet, and pretends that it is Hialmar who is the breadwinner. Hedvig adores her father but like her mother, she treats him as a difficult child, and she continues to believe that she is loved despite the growing evidence of his selfishness and neglect.

Also in the attic, in a special basket, sits the wild duck, shot and wounded by Hakon Werle and given to Hedvig, after being rescued from the "depths of the sea" by Hakon's dog. The wounded wild duck has many resonances—most obviously, perhaps, as a symbol of the objects damaged by Hakon Werle and given to the Ekdal family to look after.

Gregers becomes the Ekdals' lodger, and his passion for truth grows as he sees the make-believe world they inhabit. He invites his old friend Hialmar for a long walk, in the course of which he reveals Gina's secret liaison with his father and the dubious motives for his support of the family. He has embarked on his mission to rescue Hialmar from a life based on illusion to one founded on truth.

Gregers has always been an idealist, and he expects Hialmar to have identical views, which would lead him to embrace the truth, accept what has happened, and rebuild his marriage on a new, sound footing. However, Hialmar is nothing like Gregers, and when he discovers Gina's past and the support that Hakon has secretly provided, he reacts with righteous indignation: he is determined to leave the family and to return everything that he has received from Hakon Werle. In his rejection of everything he has been given he even tells his daughter, Hedvig, that he would like to strangle the wild duck and that the only thing that prevents him from doing so is that he knows how much it would upset her.

Another blow to Hialmar's pride takes the form of a letter from Hakon Werle that contains a deed of gift, which Hialmar tears up in a rage when he learns that it provides a pension for Old Ekdal until his death, and after that for Hedvig. However, the final blow comes when he begins to recognise that Hedvig may not be his daughter. It becomes clear that Hakon is himself going blind, and this creates the conviction in Hialmar that Hedvig's blindness is hereditary, and that Gina was already pregnant when she married him. Gina confesses her affair and admits that she cannot be sure who Hedvig's father is. Hialmar's collapse becomes most poignant when he rejects Hedvig and calls her an interloper.

Gradually, however, Hialmar allows himself to lean on Gina once more, and as he begins to feel less righteous and more needy he glues together the fragments of the torn letter so that the legacy need not be rejected. When he hears that Hedvig intends to sacrifice her precious wild duck to demonstrate her love for him, his rejection of her also softens—but it is too late, because the drama comes to its tragically fatal conclusion when Hedvig, instead of shooting the wild duck, shoots herself. She has come to believe that it is she who is the burden on her family, having been damaged by Hakon Werle and shunned by her father.

A voice of reason appears in the form of Dr Relling, who recognises Gregers' disturbance saying, "But one disease he has certainly got in his system. .... He is suffering from an acute attack of integrity" (Ibsen, 1884, pp. 71–72). Dr Relling has been trying to support Hialmar despite his illusions because he argues that, "Rob the average man of his life-illusions and you take away his happiness at the same stroke" (p. 100). Gregers has failed to recognise that Hialmar is an average man, and he has no understanding of his feelings. Moreover, Gregers's motivation for revealing what he did had less to do with Hialmar's happiness than with the wish to expose the alleged wrongdoing of his father. Gregers's hatred arises in part from his idealisation of his mother and his denial of her paranoia and alcoholism, which led to her husband's alienation and hastened her death. This means that the truth Gregers wants to impose does not take into account the wider picture and is equally based on illusion.

E M Forster and the need for kindness

In *The Wild Duck*, Ibsen forcefully reminds us that truth can be cruel and that we can become blind to the tragic consequences of its impact. The tragedy raises the importance of feelings such as pity and kindness as these are evoked in the audience who are made aware of Gregers's inability to feel them.

E M Forster pointed out that it is not simply that truth without kindness can be cruel, but that truth without kindness is not fully true. When we engage in an empathic identification with the patient we can feel the cruelty that truth inflicts and when we extricate ourselves we have to consider if the cruelty was really necessary. In *A Passage to India* (1924), where he described his heroine to have felt only cold justice and honesty and no passion of love for those whom she had wronged the similarity to Gregers is clear. Forster asserted that the truth is not really true unless it is accompanied by kindness.

Nevertheless, we also know that truth is essential for our mental health and that pursuing truth is one of the basic goals of psychoanalysis. We find ourselves in agreement with Freud when he asserts that

> we must not forget that the analytic relationship is based on a love of truth—that is, on a recognition of reality—and that it precludes any kind of sham or deceit
>
> (1937, p. 248)

Moreover, in *The Wild Duck*, Gregers's view of the benefits of truthfulness is close to that held by psychoanalysts in their model of healthy development. We argue that facing the reality of loss allows us to mourn our lost objects, to recognise our guilt, and to repair the damage we have done. What we sometimes forget is that, in order for guilt to be accepted and to motivate us toward reparation, it has to be bearable—and this is often the critical factor, as it proves to be for Hialmar. As we relinquish and mourn our illusions, we must also relinquish and mourn our omnipotence; paradoxically, this means that facing reality includes an acceptance of our limitations, including the limits to the reality we can accept.

Freud recognised that a love of truth is not the same as an idealisation of truth. He was very aware that we all need defences and that neurotic compromises are part of ordinary existence. In his words:

> It is not his [the analyst's] business to restrict himself in every situation
> in life to being a fanatic in favour of health.... We must allow that in
> some cases that flight [into illness] is fully justified, and a physician who
> has recognized how the situation lies will silently and solicitously
> withdraw.
>
> (1917, p. 382)

Freud was a great admirer of Ibsen, and in relating one of his own dreams,
he described one of his sentences as, "written in a positively *norekdal* style"
(1900, p. 296). He concluded that *norekdal* was a condensation of *Nora* and
Ekdal—the first a character in *A Doll's House* (Ibsen, 1879) and the second
in *The Wild Duck*. In discussing this dream, Anthi (1990) suggests that, at
the time, Freud was beginning to become aware that his studies in hysteria
were exposing him to criticism from his colleagues, and that, in identification with Old Ekdal, he feared humiliation and disgrace. Anthi also suggests that Freud's partnership with Fliess was coming to an end, and that
the imprisonment of Old Ekdal reminded him of his guilt about their dangerous collaboration in the case of Emma Eckstein (Masson, 1984).[3]
I suspect, however, that Freud was also becoming aware that, in his treatment of hysterical patients, he had been exerting pressure on them *to accept
the truth*, and that the portrayal of Gregers in *The Wild Duck* may have
alerted him to the harm that can be done by overzealous idealists.

   Freud could recognise both the value of truth and the dangers of an
insensitive imposition of it on others, and this capacity to entertain contradictory points of view, is the essential feature of irony. I will discuss irony in
later chapters, especially Chapter 10 and here only comment that Gregers's
concrete solution to the problem shows that he is completely without
a capacity for irony. This means that he cannot extricate himself from an
identification with Hialmar; hence he cannot observe what he has done or
feel pity for those whom he has exposed. He cannot feel tolerance or kindness toward them and is intent only on taking action that is unrestrained by
thought or self-doubt.

The analyst as zealot

A determination to expose the truth can become a passion and lead to
a righteous attitude on the part of the analyst that ignores the subjective
experience of the patient and because of that can distort and misrepresent
the overall reality the patient is having to face. Just as Gregers was exposed
as having an agenda of his own in exacting revenge upon his father, the
analyst may have ulterior motives which have more to do with his own identity problems and his own struggle with envy and jealousy. We have seen
that utopian visions represent a dangerous idealisation of the aims of any
philosophy because in these cases the ideal is treated as if it were concretely
realisable rather than a symbol of excellence. In these cases the rebellious

side of the analyst may be split off and projected into his patient where it is pressured to conform to what is held to be reality.

I have argued that an important safeguard in these cases arises from a sense of irony which constantly reminds us of something ridiculous and comic in our attitude and that this can act as a safeguard that prevents us from taking ourselves too seriously. Both Gregers and his counterpart Hialmar are quite unable to adopt an ironic stance and they take everything seriously and concretely. What a relief it is to find Dr. Relling, who recognises that Gregers suffers "from an acute attack of integrity". Relling can use irony and expresses a deeper sense of truth when he understands that Hialmar needs his illusions as we all do. I believe that with the help of irony the patient feels that the analyst is a fellow sufferer and that together a gradual appreciation of the value of truth can be set alongside a need for illusion.

Notes

1 Based in part on Steiner, J. (2016) Illusion, Disillusion, and Irony in Psychoanalysis. *Psychoanalytic Quarterly*, 85, 427–447.
2 This situation is similar to that described by Racker (1957) who differentiates concordant from complementary identifications.
3 Other analysts have recognised the importance of *The Wild Duck* in understanding the complex relationship we have with reality. Anthi (1990), Killingmo (1994), and Szalita (1970–1971) have contributed interesting papers on the play's relevance to psychoanalysis, and Zachrisson (2013) explored the search for truth and the need for illusion in both *The Wild Duck* (Ibsen, 1884) and *Oedipus the King* (Sophocles, 5th century BC).

4　The use and abuse of omnipotence in the journey of the hero[1]

Generally speaking omnipotence, with its magical solutions to realistic problems, is considered an obstacle to development and is often the driving force behind narcissistic phantasies that underlie pathological organisations. These organisations create obstacles to progress in analysis and it is generally understood that for development to proceed they must be relinquished in accord with the dictates of reality. However, the contrary need, that is to espouse and enjoy omnipotence, is rarely recognised and not usually viewed as an action that could be to the patient's advantage. We are used to thinking of omnipotence as a bad thing, indicative of madness and loss of control and we sometimes fail to understand how important it is to be ready to engage in omnipotent phantasy and even to put such phantasies into action.

In this chapter I will describe how omnipotent phantasies can not only help us to escape from the paralysis of depression and the despair of helplessness but may form the basis of the rebellion against conventional constraints that are necessary if new developments are to proceed. Klein supported the idea that mania as well as depression was part of early development and stated that omnipotence may,

> enable the early ego to assert itself to a certain degree against its internal persecutors and against a slavish and perilous dependence upon its loved objects...

> (Klein, 1940, p. 349)

In her last paper, published after her death, "On the sense of loneliness" she described how omnipotence lessens with "integration and a growing sense of reality", but that this lessening leads to a "diminished capacity for hope". Hopefulness and confidence may be more secure if they are based on achievement but "an element of omnipotence is always part of it" (Klein, 1963, pp. 304–305).

I believe that in the course of development, both in life and in analysis, omnipotence must be initially embraced and subsequently relinquished. This is particularly important in the struggle over power as the developing child emancipates himself from his early dependence on his parents. This situation is relived in an analysis as the patient struggles to establish his own identity and it is also a prominent aspect of the creative artist, scientist, or explorer, who must be willing to challenge prevailing views if he is to explore new ground. In all these situations the individual can only break away from restrictive influences if he is willing to engage in omnipotent phantasies and embark on omnipotent projects. A bid towards independence that over-throws established authority is unconsciously experienced as an oedipal murder and further progress in which the initial omnipotence is recognised and relinquished involves a painful working through of the Oedipus Complex.

The need both to espouse and then to relinquish omnipotence is charac-teristic of the journey of the hero and I will use Joseph Campbell's (1949), descriptions to examine the difficult task by which the hero, whether he is a scientist, a toddler or a patient, can both adopt omnipotence and also relinquish it to find his way back to reality.

The journey of the hero

Joseph Campbell in his now-famous book, *The Hero with a Thousand Faces* (1949), describes a universal structure of myths in which the hero travels from the known world into the unknown; there he faces challenges and temptations, and engages in battles with superhuman forces. In his struggles the hero sometimes derives hope and assurance from a helpful female figure, by whose magic he is protected, but eventually he is let down, defeated, and descends into an abyss connected with death and despair. Heroically he picks himself up and taking advantage of his descent into des-pair he is able to gain important self-knowledge, sometimes, for example, through a visit to the underworld. This knowledge makes him powerful and allows him to recover the confidence to embark on further adventures. However, his wish to return to his home in the world of ordinary mortals begins to assert itself and to return he must agree to relinquish omnipo-tence. Such relinquishment is always difficult and involves further trials cen-tring on a capacity to relate to forces more powerful than he is. Campbell sees this as a need for "atonement with the father" and in this task the hero again usually needs the help of a female figure so that he can survive the anticipated power of the threatening father. If he is able to face and to submit to this power and relinquish his omnipotence he can return to the real world, sometimes with a gift to bestow on mankind. Campbell himself likens the hero's journey to the inner journey we are obliged to make in order to understand ourselves.

If the hero fails to embark on his adventures he is not really a hero at all; he remains an ordinary mortal, perhaps ashamed of his cowardice or per-haps simply recognising his limitations. He conforms to the habits, the dogma, and prejudice of his time and is unable to break new ground. His failure to rebel denies him the experience of life-enhancing adventures, such as those involving heroic battles leading to both victories and defeats. The true hero has the capacity to tackle adventures even if they seem to be grandiose and he has to be willing to suffer the defeats that failure brings.

At other times the hero is able to begin in truly heroic fashion but is unable to give up omnipotence and return to the ordinary world. If he remains unrepentant and determined to hold onto omnipotence he is trapped in the world of unrealistic phantasy where power leads either to triumph and superiority or to defeat and humiliation. The hero who cannot relinquish and mourn his omnipotence is a failed hero, and such failure is often a step towards becoming a villain. Indeed, the persistent belief in omnipotent prowess is likely to become the core of a delusional system inflicting humiliation with unrestrained cruelty.

The situation that the hero finds himself in as he recovers from defeats is critical. Sometimes the recovery leads to a return to heroic battles and renewed searching for triumph and revenge, but the true hero, unlike the villain, is determined to return home to the world of ordinary mortals. He has the courage to relinquish omnipotence and to acknowledge the reality of his place in a human family.

Separation-individuation in the development of the child

In order to embark on and then return from his quest the hero must first acquire and subsequently relinquish omnipotence, and I think we can see the same pattern in the observations of Margaret Mahler (1972, 1974, Mahler, Pine, and Bergman, 1975), of toddlers beginning to walk. In her research Mahler was impressed by how, towards the end of his first year, the infant begins to explore and to become delighted and excited by his new achievements. He is not only pleased but wants to show off his new-found skills, embarking on what Mahler refers to as his "love affair with the world". This is the *practising phase* of a series of developmental stages making up the separation–individuation cycle, in the course of which the infant gradually develops a sense of separateness from his mother. In the practising phase the toddlers enjoy an elated preoccupation with locomotion and exploration, and become so thrilled with their performance that they do not even mind if they fall over or bump into things. They are unashamedly exhibitionistic and narcissistic but as observers we share their pleasure and do not begrudge them their excitement. Indeed we can see the germs of the hero in the toddler embarking on his adventures even if we are aware that his confidence is based on identifications with powerful objects that help to conceal a reality of smallness and dependence.

Sadly, it doesn't last, and the phase of narcissistic confidence is followed by a *rapprochement crisis* set off by the collapse of the illusion of omnipotence. Pine, one of Mahler's colleagues concludes, "Now he is small and alone in a big world, rather than sharing in the (imagined) omnipotence of the mother—child unit" (Pine, 1980, p. 226). The crisis introduces the *rapprochement sub-phase* in which the infant once again stays close to his mother and becomes anxious when his physical mobility leads to a sense of separateness from her. The toddler becomes tentative, wanting his mother to be in sight so that he can gain reassurance through eye contact and is evidently in conflict between staying with his mother and being more independent. Mahler observed that, if the mother reacts with impatience or unavailability a fear of abandonment may arise in the toddler.

In the past Mahler's observations were mostly neglected by Kleinian analysts in part perhaps because of a reaction against Mahler's earlier view, later amended, that in the first few weeks of life the baby was detached and self-absorbed in an autistic state and made no object relations (Mahler, 1974). This meant that it was difficult to trace the stages in the separation-individuation cycle back to early infantile experience.

Subsequently, however, just as with the Oedipus Complex, it became possible to see early precursors of the various stages Mahler described, and indeed, some of the observations she made of toddlers have parallels in observations of babies only a few weeks old[2]. Initially it was also difficult to link Mahler's observations made of children in a day nursery to the analyst's experience in the analytic setting, but this too has changed as I hope to show in this paper. Indeed we recognise that separation-individuation is a critical issue for development in analysis even though we tend to use different terms to describe the process. In particular we are now much more aware that disillusionments from idealised phantasies commonly occur in analysis and have a very precise parallel with the disillusion described by Mahler as a rapprochement crisis.

Once we recognise these parallels we can use Mahler's observations to alert us to some of the detailed anxieties, excitements, and disappointments that patients experience in the course of their analyses as they go through the process of relinquishing their omnipotence and begin to forge a separate identity. One of these features of the struggle for separateness is that embarrassment, shame, and humiliation may become prominent as a protective pathological organisation is relinquished. I have thought of this in terms of a sensitivity to being seen as patients begin to emerge from a psychic retreat (Steiner, 2011), and was struck by similar experiences that are described in relation to the rapprochement crisis.

Mahler described how the toddler expects his sense of self-admiration to be met by a similar state in the mother leading to a confirmation of a shared omnipotence (Mahler, 1972, 1974, Schore, 1991). Instead of a maternal smile of confirmation there is the shock of deflation as the child is confronted with a mother who lets him down, sometimes in a catastrophic manner. She may be preoccupied with a sibling, her husband, or another rival, or she may simply not share the child's wonderment and excitement with his achievement. If he is not confirmed as a hero he feels himself to be nothing, and the fall is associated with feelings of collapse, shame and humiliation.

Of course, the deflation is a step towards relinquishing illusion and facing reality but if it is too sudden and unexpected the infant is shattered. This is especially so if the grandiosity and exhibitionism have been extreme and the gap between success and failure is too great. Similar crises may follow future deflations of narcissism and these occasions can be difficult for mothers and their children as well as for analysts and their patients. It is the mother's failure to admire that produces the deflation and the hateful attacks it provokes from the infant may make it difficult for her to see that the child is in special need of her support. Winnicott has proposed that,

> The mother's eventual task is gradually to disillusion the infant, but she has no hope of success unless at first she has been able to give sufficient opportunity for illusion.
>
> (1953, p. 95)

I take this to mean that the infant must be allowed the pleasure of the practising phase and then supported through the rapprochement crisis. I think it is possible to compare the stages in the journey of the infant towards independence to that of the hero. Indeed, there is something heroic in the toddler's excited and omnipotent voyage of exploration and, like the hero, the toddler has to survive the descent into an abyss of despair and dejection when the omnipotence collapses. As with the hero the outcome of the infant's journey depends on what happens next. Can the infant recover his confidence? Is this based on a resumption of omnipotence or can he return to the real world, bringing back the lessons he has learned. As he deals with the aftermath of the rapprochement crisis the infant faces tests of his capacity to relinquish omnipotence and mourn it. If mourning is successful he is strengthened to endure the ordinary discomforts of reality, including those of shame and humiliation, a degree of which is inevitable in the course of achieving separateness.

We are aware clinically how central it is for the analyst to support the patient in surviving these experiences and to help him to resist a return to the omnipotent world of conflicts over power. This final struggle in his return to the non-omnipotent world of ordinary human endeavour involves a deference to the reality of difference and hierarchy similar to Campbell's "atonement with the father". As with the hero, a great deal will depend on the mother's capacity and willingness to help her infant regain his place in a family where he can be loved.

Disillusionment in the consulting room

These kinds of experience portrayed in myths and described in observational studies have their counterpart in psychoanalytic observations made in the consulting room. While disillusionments are inevitable and universal, the way these are handled by the patient, and by the analyst, can have a critical effect on the outcome. If the shame and humiliation accompanying the deflation are too painful to bear the patient feels rebuffed and rejected and may come to believe that, if he is not admired, he can no longer be loved. He loses confidence in his capacity to love and be loved, and he strives to re-establish an omnipotence in order to deal with humiliation by inflicting it on others. In this way a conflict over power replaces the conflict over love and leads to cycles of triumph and humiliation where issues of power and dominance override all other considerations.

I want to look at these situations and try to trace them to what I have come to think of as clinical rapprochement crises through which the hero attempts to return to the real world and restore his place in the family. This sometimes happens when the hero is defeated and sometimes when he longs to restore his relationship with his good objects and find love rather than admiration. I will examine some of these issues in clinical material in which I have in mind a parallel between the patient's journeys with those of a hero.

Clinical material. Mr A[3]

I am now going to take a fresh look at some old clinical material (Steiner, 2011). The material comes from the analysis of a patient who embarked on innumerable projects very similar to the adventures of the heroes of mythology. Even though the projects had a grandiose flavour they had some creative potential and several got off the ground with the support of one or other patron in his field of business. Then when his project failed, usually after some initial success, he collapsed into a period of extreme anxiety accompanied by somatic symptoms chiefly of joint and muscle pain. He sought the help of numerous doctors and pressured them to embark on what seemed to be dangerous and heroic treatments and put enormous pressure on me to agree that immediate relief was imperative. Gradually his panic gave way to dejection and after a period of despair and self-recrimination he typically picked himself up and resumed his quest, having, for the most part, learned little from the experience. Each new project held the same promise to achieve great things and to my mind was fuelled by the same omnipotent phantasy designed to transform humiliation into triumph in order to regain his rightful place alongside an ideal object. Marital problems accompanied his failures and his need for a business triumph was linked to the belief that, to have him back, success is what his wife demanded. At times of failure he felt humiliated and wronged and his primary goal was to get me to agree that he had been treated unfairly.

If I failed to support his ambition he saw me as dislodging him from his place as a partner in an ideal couple and adopting that place for myself. This provoked a renewed experience of humiliation and a renewed accusation of unfairness. The predominant complaint was one of injustice, and Mr A's failure to find the support from me that he sought, engendered an indignant incomprehension and resentment.

Gradually, following many such experiences, he established a business with more modest goals and more in keeping with his resources. His anxiety lessened, the somatic pain was no longer mentioned, and he was more able to examine what usually happened in his attempts to restore both his business and his marriage. The improvement allowed us to talk about ending his analysis and, especially after we had decided on a termination date about a year hence, a calmer atmosphere prevailed. A new development was the emergence of sadness; for example when he contemplated ending the analysis and wondered what it would be like not to come to his session every morning.

Mr A often extended breaks by taking holidays or business trips of his own. There were fewer such trips in recent months but some two months before the termination date, he decided to accept an invitation to give a talk at a business convention in Germany, which would necessitate missing a Friday session.

The first session: the collapse of the ideal of a helpful father

On the Thursday session immediately before this business trip, Mr A began by launching into a description of what he called a very difficult situation. His wife had suggested that he might help his son to find a job. He was in a position to do so through business contacts and he had avoided this previously thinking that his son could manage on his own and that he might be accused of pulling strings. He described that, at the cost of considerable effort, and also feeling uncertain if it was right, he had followed his wife's suggestion and arranged some possible contacts, which he sent to his son in an email. This had led to disaster. Instead of winning approval from his son and his wife the patient received an angry email in which he was accused of interfering and of trampling on his son's independence. At this point in the session what he had earlier described as a difficult situation had become a catastrophe. He insisted that he was a terrible failure, that there was something wrong with his thinking, that wires were connected up wrongly in his head, and that he was beyond being saved. Moreover, he decided that this failure must be a revenge for the feeling of complacency he had felt in recent weeks, when things had been going deceptively well. He had felt good about a directors' meeting at work, and about his relationship with his wife, with whom he had relaxed in the garden over the weekend. He had gazed with pride at the work he had done on the stone patio, the flower-beds, and the water feature, which all looked nice. It had made him think that he had built things up again and re-established a better link with his wife. Now he re-iterated that he had pulled the rug out from under himself and everything had come crashing down.

I linked the patient's description of disaster with his anxiety over the business trip he was to take to Germany the next day, and interpreted that he was trying to persuade me that if I didn't join him in his excitement of what he could do in Germany and support him as a father should support a son, everything would collapse. In the course of the session I pointed out his uncertainty as to how a father might best support a son. I suggested that although he did feel we had done some useful analytic work he knew it was far from complete and far from perfect and it left him unsure how solid the relationship with me was. He seemed afraid that everything between us could collapse and that he would be thrown into an abyss of despair and self-recrimination and I think was relieved that I did not make a big issue of his trip to Germany. Mr A seemed to listen, but nevertheless continued to insist that the disaster was real. He went on repeating that just as he had built up something better with his wife and felt he had a family and a home it all collapsed and he now felt he had lost everything.

Discussion

It seemed to me that the situation between the patient, his wife, and his son, was the enactment of a phantasy that his trip to Germany was a heroic adventure that he expected me to admire, like the work he had done in the garden. Even my neutral stance was felt as a failure to confirm what was meant as a triumph over a father figure in order to regain his position as his mother's admired partner. This fitted with repeated attempts to get me to stand down as a father and accept that he should take my place. When I treated the business trip as something he could make his own judgements on he felt I was failing to confirm his superiority. Now I thought he was describing a crisis in which he collapsed into an abyss of ruin and recrimination. These periods of collapse were familiar and at the point of crisis he was probably right that the "wires were connected up wrongly in his head" and that "he was beyond being saved" because he seriously believed that he had a defect in his capacity to understand himself and his objects, which I could not put right. However, at other points in the session he seemed to have quite a bit of insight. Until persuaded of the contrary by his wife he had confidence in his son and believed that pulling strings was wrong, and he was able to question his own omnipotence both in solving his son's career problems and in repairing his marriage through some work in the garden.

The next session: regrets and sadness

After the weekend in Germany, Mr A came back on Monday pleased that his talk had gone well and relieved that his son was no longer angry. In a long, warm, and apologetic email, his son told him much more of his feelings and plans. However, his son now complained that the patient's aunt, who had given him some money, was trying to control him through expressing an interest in how he used it. The patient was surprised because this aunt was very generous and for him had been an ally against his father. He had always been curious why it was this aunt and not his father who took him camping when he was a boy. Then, while watching a television documentary about D-Day, he felt a wave of sympathy towards his father who had taken part in the landings in Normandy and fought through northern France to Germany. He thought that perhaps camping with his son might have been too reminiscent of the dangers and anxieties of the war.

I interpreted that the improved relationship he had established with me—perhaps in part because I did not collapse on Thursday—had helped him to enjoy the weekend. He could partly accept that I did not want to go with him on some of his projects but he could go on his own perhaps supported by my confidence in his ability to make his own choices.

Mr A replied that he had some thoughts about Germany, and reminded me that some of the tension in his family lay between his mother, who admired Germany, and his father, who, because of his bitter experiences in the war, had an antipathy to all things German and idealised the French. On the weekend the Germans were impressed by his talk, and he felt a wave of excitement. Now he wondered if he sided with his mother against his father.

I suggested that the patient might think that I, and psychoanalysis as well, had a history connected with the war and consequently that, like his parents, I might take sides. He said that he realised that the Germans had annexed Austria and that psychoanalysis was Austrian and Jewish. He himself had had always wanted to study at Heidelberg. Then he remembered one remarkable day when he had been sitting in a café in Germany, near the French border. He had had a good meal and some wine and wrote what began as some notes for a business venture he was planning. As he wrote he realised that his writing was being transformed into a personal manifesto. It was long and involved, but it had flowed easily and he remembered being very impressed with it. But now he had the thought that if he were to look at it, he might see it as nonsense.

After a silence, his anger returned and he complained that he felt controlled by his father who was always trying to cut him down to size. Even the plants in his garden had to be pruned in order to keep them in their place. Then in a sadder mood he returned to the documentary about the D-Day landings. On the television they had mentioned that this would be the last programme of its kind because soon there would be no veterans left. I interpreted that he was now more aware of the end of the analysis, which linked to a time when I would no longer be here. This created a conflict. He could easily see me as controlling and as demanding he submit to my authority. Then, if he rebelled, he expected a terrible collapse unless he could defeat me. He said, yes, it was a manic sort of freedom and dangerous. He knew it was connected with fascism and power. He said that he realised that his father was getting older and he would not be there to see what use he had made of his inheritance. He said he thought that his son was wrong to worry about being controlled by his aunt. She was generous and she gave him money knowing that she would not be there to see how it was spent.

I suggested that he was more aware of having regrets. He did get resentful when he felt that I cut him down to size, but that now he was less convinced that his actions and phantasies would lead to a catastrophic loss of love and to a collapse. He had become excited when his phantasies involved an alliance with powerful forces but he was not so certain now that one of us had to triumph and destroy the other. Instead he was more aware of my age and of the ending of the analysis, and he felt freer to make use of what he gained from it when he realised that in the future I would not be there to control him.

Discussion

I found it useful to consider the patient's business projects as heroic adventures in which he formed an alliance with an admiring figure, usually his mother, who sustained his omnipotence by confirming his superiority. When he failed to impress his wife, his son, or his business associates he collapsed into anxiety and chaos. The dominant demand he made on me was to offer him praise and admiration in order to sustain his omnipotence, and when I failed to do this he felt humiliated and blamed me for cutting him down to size and making him feel small. After a period of chaotic anxiety and self-recrimination he was able to pick himself up and recover some self-esteem. However, it was always finely balanced as to whether he resumed his omnipotent attempts to recover his superiority or whether he could learn from the experience and find sufficient satisfaction of a more ordinary kind.

In the session I have reported he became superior and triumphant when the German audience admired his ideas, and he was reminded of the manifesto he wrote in the café on the French-German border, which he connected with a sense of freedom and power in alliance with powerful fascist figures. In this omnipotent phantasy success was based on an alliance with a German loving mother against a French loving father, but ultimately involved phantasies of destroying both parents in images connected with Nazi power and cruelty. This made reparation impossible and gave rise to despair and self-recrimination.

Challenges for the hero if he wishes to return

To move from the omnipotent world of power, triumph, and humiliation to return to the ordinary world of human scale and endeavour involves two challenges. First the omnipotence must be relinquished and mourned and second the relationship with the primary object must be resumed. Both give rise to difficulties. Before we can relinquish omnipotence we have to recognise how much pleasure it gives us and, especially when erotised, how addictive a hold it can have on the personality. Paradoxically this seems to be true even when defeats and humiliations are repeatedly experienced, perhaps because of masochistic gratification but also, I think, because defeat gives rise to renewed phantasies of triumph and recovery. Relinquishment involves saying goodbye to these exciting ups and downs, and the loss is painful and has to be acknowledged and mourned.

However, the second challenge, namely that of returning to the ordinary world, also presents problems usually quite similar to those that led to the rapprochement crisis in the first place. Even if we are able to return to a place in the family that is neither omnipotently inflated nor catastrophically reduced, we are left with the need to renegotiate the relationship with our primary objects. This means that we are obliged to tolerate feelings of need and dependence and it is these that create special difficulties.

In his analysis my patient often restated his longing to come home to an ordinary family, and like Odysseus he never lost the yearning for his wife and home. However, this return, and the relinquishing of omnipotence that went with it, seemed to demand a special form of courage. To support him through this part of his journey required sensitivity to a tenderness within him that initially he found effeminate and unacceptable. My patient would often repeat how intolerable it was for him to see his father put his arm around his mother's shoulder, insisting that it made him cringe. Like Satan he could not bear to see them, "imparidised in one another's arms", and he denied that this could be a genuine expression of affection. Later he came to think that, although flawed, his parents' relationship did have loving moments, and it was clear that it was precisely such affectionate gestures that he longed to be able to enjoy with his wife. Returning home to a world without omnipotence involved the de-idealisation of this kind of scene and perceiving it as more ordinary meant that it did not seem quite as false and cringe-making.

The hallmarks of a true hero: recognising the failure of omnipotence and returning to reality

Of course, these formulations about the trajectory of the hero mostly apply to men although women too may identify with powerful male figures. In Chapter 7 I describe how the feelings of smallness and dependence that arise after the relinquishment of omnipotence may lead to an idealisation of phallic masculinity because of the wish to restore the idealisation through the exercise of power. However, a good example of feminine heroism can be seen in the rebellion of Eve against the restraints imposed on her in the Garden of Eden. She had the courage to defy God's prohibition against knowledge when she allowed herself to be seduced into attempting to equal

God in his omnipotence. The fact that she failed and had to submit to reality does not in my view diminish her heroism because she was also courageous enough to face reality and transform her view of God from that of a tyrannical father to that of an ideal symbol. I described this in Chapter 2 where I also contrasted her fate with that of Satan, whom we might consider as a failed hero. In his former embodiment as Lucifer he had been able to rebel against what seemed to be cruel and unjust demands. Instead of submitting to the authority of Christ whose arrival in Heaven dethroned him just as a child feels dethroned by a new baby, Satan withdrew in resentment and at the head of an army of his followers, unleashed the war in Heaven that eventually led to his defeat and expulsion. His rebellion against what he must have realised were impossible odds was truly heroic but subsequently, after his fall, he was unable to repent, to return to the real world and to see God as a symbol of goodness rather than as a cruel authority.

Notes

1 Based on Steiner, J. (2015). The Use and Abuse of Omnipotence in the Journey of the Hero. *Psychoanalytic Quarterly*, 84, 695–718.
2 For example, Murray and Trevarthen (1985), filmed sessions in which they asked mothers to talk to their infants while they viewed each other through a TV link. A lively interaction took place in which it was often the baby that set the pace and the mother who followed. If the communication was interfered with however, these babies became profoundly disturbed and indeed seemed to collapse. Their faces fell and they became bewildered and distraught. This occurred if the mothers were asked abruptly to stop playing and to put on a deadpan face, or equally so if the interaction was de-synchronised by introducing a delay between the baby's gestures and the mother's response. Murray later linked these findings to disturbances in the babies of non-responsive depressed mothers and it seems to me that it represents an early version of a rapprochement crisis.
3 Material from this patient are presented in Steiner (2011) and other sessions are discussed in Chapter 7.

5 Disillusion, humiliation, and perversion of the facts of life[1]

In this chapter the importance of humiliation in disillusion is examined. We have seen that the loss of the ideal can be felt as a shock, as a punishment, and as a trauma but above all it is felt as a humiliation. When the individual is suddenly confronted with the facts of life he is brought up against a variety of differences between others and between himself and others, differences that have been avoided in the illusion of idealisation. Prominent amongst these are feelings of inferiority because disillusion is always experienced as a fall downwards from a state of perfection to an inferior position and humiliation is part of that experience of tumbling downwards. The baby who a moment before felt exalted and perfect now feels small and dirty as the protective cloak of idealisation is removed.

In my previous work on emerging from a psychic retreat I described how "seeing" and "being seen" become possible and that the first and most immediate consequence is a feeling of being exposed and naked (Steiner, 2011). The new situation without the protection of the retreat introduces the subject to the shame of inferiority and when he believes that he is looked down on he feels humiliated.

It is true that as well as feeling himself to be "seen" the subject is able to observe others and this "seeing" may give him the opportunity to view life as it is and eventually to accommodate to it. "Seeing" provides an opportunity to observe the state of our objects and because this means viewing the damage we have done, guilt has to be faced. The feelings of guilt may also be difficult to bear and are usually felt to be deeper and more serious than those of humiliation. However the need to reverse humiliation is more urgent and this means that a proper consideration of guilt and access to mourning and reparation is delayed until the humiliation has been accepted and worked through. When they *can* be worked through, as I shall spell out below, it is possible for the patient to proceed along the path that leads via mourning to reparation. Hence although both "seeing" and "being seen" are consequences of disillusion the benefits of "seeing" cannot be enjoyed until problems of "being seen", with the consequent humiliation, have been experienced and survived.

The emphasis on humiliation appears in myth and fairy tale such as the story of the Emperor's new clothes which shows the shame inflicted when a narcissistic phantasy of superiority collapses to reveal the nakedness that had been clothed by illusion.[2] In *Paradise Lost* the fall from perfection is accompanied by feelings of shame as Adam and Eve become embarrassed at their nakedness and I will argue that the capacity to feel and tolerate humiliation was important in their rehabilitation. As we shall see the fall of Lucifer, by contrast, led to a defiance because for him the humiliation was unbearable.

The difference between acceptance of reality and submission to authority

In some circumstances the facts of life impinge from the impact of ordinary events in the real world as is the case of accidental falls and natural disasters. These may have a traumatic effect but are nevertheless easier to accept than is the case when the trauma appears to be imposed through the agency of another person with a malign intention. However, because even a benign environment can inflict hurt, it is often difficult to tell if the malign intention is real or phantasied. The prototype of disillusion arises when the mother shares her love and attention with others and this may be experienced as a betrayal and a humiliation as was the case with Klein's child patient Erna who believed that,

> ... any expression of her mother's tenderness towards her father had one chief purpose, which was to arouse the child's envy and to wound its feelings
>
> (Klein, 1932, p. 46)

Whether the insult is real or imagined the fall is humiliating and is felt as a betrayal so that the hurt makes it difficult for the child to accept that he is loved and has a rightful place in the family.

Sometimes the rebellion against authority is initiated by the child as a bid for freedom and independence and in these cases the fall from grace is less humiliating. From this point of view Eve emerges as the true heroine of *Paradise Lost* when she challenges the authority of God and demands the right of access to knowledge for herself and for Adam. Acquiring knowledge meant that she and Adam were aware that they had done wrong and the feelings of shame made them wish to hide and cover their nakedness. However the humiliation was not so great that recovery was impossible. Milton makes a sharp contrast with Satan who as we shall see was so humiliated that there was no way back. It does seem that the degree of humiliation is an important factor in determining whether recovery from the trauma of disillusion is possible or not.

Humiliation and hierarchy

The ability to humiliate is an important factor in determining hierarchy within the family and within society. Differences that arise as a consequence of the facts of life mean that we each have a place determined by our capacities. A universal hierarchy such as "The Great Chain of Being" discussed in Chapter 2, may function as a stabilising factor when the position occupied is felt to reflect reality but is often a cause of resentment if an individual feels displaced from their rightful position through the exercise of power. If the loss of a place in the family hierarchy is felt to be unjust and cruel it is felt as a humiliation and is particularly likely to provoke phantasies of resentment and revenge. The humiliation of groups and even of nations that commonly follows a defeat is a powerful motivator of revenge leading to conflict and war.

Perversions as misrepresentations of the facts of life

Because of the importance of humiliation the capacity to survive this experience is critical in determining to what extent normal relations can be resumed. When supportive figures are able to persuade the patient that damage to his pride does not signify catastrophe a return to normal relations in the family may result, but if this does not happen then thwarted desire can turn to hatred: revenge is then sought through attempts to inflict the humiliation onto someone else. In pursuit of this aim reality is misrepresented and especially the distinction between good and evil is distorted.

It is interesting to note that the early meaning of the term perverse referred to the "Distortion or corruption of the original course, meaning, or state of something", and only much later to "Sexual behaviour that is considered abnormal and unacceptable" (OED).

To pervert meant:　1. To turn upside down; to upset; to subvert 1656.
　　　　　　　　　　2. To turn aside from its right course, aim, meaning.
　　　　　　　　　　3. *trans.* To turn (a person, the mind, etc.) away from right opinion or action; to lead astray; to corrupt.

Initially what was true and good was defined in religious terms and the opposite of perversion was conversion. However, eventually the term came to be associated with sexual excitement and it does seem to be the case that misrepresentations of the facts of life commonly form the basis of perverse phantasies and daydreams.

The compromise formation in Freud's descriptions of fetishism

Freud discusses a special instance of the conflict between the ideal and the real in his description of the child's reaction to gender difference. He described how the child initially denies the difference of gender and prefers to believe that his mother has a penis just as his father does. His observations and reasoning put him in touch with the real situation which however is neither accepted nor denied. Both the original belief *and the* new evidence based on observation are retained, sometimes aided by a spurious justification which Freud believed developed into a special way of dealing with reality involving methods of reasoning that he thought "almost deserves to be described as artful" (Freud, 1938, p. 277).

He suggests that this mechanism may be responsible for the creation of a fetish.

> To put it more plainly: the fetish is a substitute for the woman's (the mother's) penis that the little boy once believed in and—for reasons familiar to us—does not want to give up. What happened, therefore, was that the boy refused to take cognizance of the fact of his having perceived that a woman does not possess a penis. No, that could not be true: for if a woman had been castrated, then his own possession of a penis was in danger; and against that there rose in rebellion the portion of his narcissism which Nature has, as a precaution, attached to that particular organ.
>
> (Freud, 1927, p. 153)

Later (Freud, 1938) attributed this way of dealing with reality to a splitting of the ego in which one part accepts the reality that is denied by the other.

> Thus there is a conflict between the demand by the instinct and the prohibition by reality. But in fact the child takes neither course, or rather he takes both simultaneously, which comes to the same thing. He replies to the conflict with two contradictory reactions, both of which are valid and effective.
>
> (p. 275)

It is this artful way of both accepting and rejecting reality that is a feature of the perverse solution to the facts of life and especially to the problem of how to deal with the humiliation inflicted by disillusion. This means that misrepresentations rather than denials of reality enable normal development to proceed alongside perverse distortions.

Romantic recreations of the Garden of Eden Illusion

Perhaps the most common reaction to disillusion is to deny that it has happened or, when this fails, to deny that it needed to happen. In this way reality is seen as an injustice and illusion retains its ideal quality if only it could be regained. Such denials are seen in the "if-only" and "someday" phantasies described in Chapter 1 (Akhtar, 1996) which assert that the Garden of Eden is not an illusion but a realisable reality and the loss might have been avoided and perfection eventually restored. As a comfort and consolation romantic phantasies of idyllic states are commonly created but now seem more obviously to misrepresent the facts of life and to reveal their superficial character. They are particularly directed against the passage of time and are described as romantic perversions below.

The transformation of thwarted desire into hatred

However when such romantic recreations are unsuccessful the failure to sustain the ideal is felt as a betrayal and the desire for the ideal object turns to phantasies of revenge. In this way relief is provided by the idea that the humiliation can be reversed and inflicted on someone else. Stoller (1987) has suggested that perverse phantasies and daydreams commonly involve a scenario which inflicts humiliation in order to deal with feelings of having been humiliated. He sees this to be an important function of pornographic phantasies and daydreams which:

> ward off and then undo the effect of humiliations that, striking from any direction, are defended against by each turn in the daydream's script.
>
> (Stoller, 1987, p. 296)

Satan unrepentant

The defiance and dedication to revenge is vividly described by Milton in *Paradise Lost* when he shows Satan as unable to relent as he expresses his hatred of God and his wish to exact his revenge with unyielding determination. Realising that God is too powerful to defeat in a direct attack he attempts and almost succeeds in his aim of seducing and destroying God's proud creation, that is Man. He is unrepentant, and defiantly proclaims that to submit to God's injustice would be wrong and shameful.

> To bow and sue for grace
> With suppliant knee, and deifie his power,
> ... that were low indeed.
>
> (Book One, 114)

For Satan it would be a weakness to admit his wrong and repent it and his hatred of God's goodness reveals how central envy is to his cause.

to be weak is miserable
Doing or Suffering: but of this be sure,
To do ought good never will be our task,
But ever to do ill our sole delight ...

(Book One, 160)

For a brief moment Satan wavers but in sadness he realises that there is no way back and it is this that leads him to espouse evil as his goal. The cruelty of disillusion has led to a despair and a disbelief that the relationship with a good object can be restored.

The facts of life and their misrepresentations

I am going to summarise Money-Kyrle's descriptions of the facts of life and then describe some of the ways these can be misrepresented. Rather arbitrarily I have suggested that misrepresentations of the first fact give rise to narcissistic perversions, those of the second fact to oedipal perversions and those of the third fact to romantic perversions. In each of these situations the first impulse seems to be to re-create the idealisation in order to undo the disillusion. When the idealisation cannot be restored thwarted desire leads to hatred which can dominate our relationship with good objects both internal and external.

Money-Kyrle describes his facts of life as follows. First, "the recognition of the breast as a supremely good object", second, "the recognition of the parents' intercourse as a supremely creative act", and third, "the recognition of the inevitability of time and ultimately death" (1971, p. 103). Each of these facts of life represent aspects of reality that are difficult to accept and they are commonly replaced by alternative versions of reality. Moreover these misrepresentations commonly become erotised and incorporated into perverse scenarios which create additional problems in analysis because of the addictive hold they can have on the personality.

The first fact: the reality of dependence on an external good object

The recognition of the breast as a supremely good object is the first and perhaps most fundamental fact of life because it establishes the new-born infant's dependence on the existence of goodness that exists outside the self. It challenges the narcissistic illusion, "The breast is a part of me, I am the breast" (Freud, 1941, p. 299), which dominates the Garden of Eden Illusion and leads to a new and initially shocking realisation of dependence on an object separate from the self.

Just as Adam had to accept the need to work and to overcome thorns and thistles in order to produce food, so the infant at the breast has to work to overcome resistance and gain access to the milk provided by the mother. The need to work is connected with the passage of time because there is an inevitable delay between the desire and its satisfaction and in contrast to the instant gratification in the Garden of Eden, waiting becomes a fact of life. Indeed, it is during the period of waiting, in the gap between the desire and the satisfaction, that the infant is subject to a huge range of emotions that centre on anxiety and pain when the good object seems to be unavailable and possibly lost. Waiting leads to feelings of smallness, immaturity and neediness in relation to the mother who seems to own all of the richness that is felt to be withheld by her.

The second fact: the reality of the parents' sexual relationship

Money-Kyrle's second fact of life is really an extension of the first because as soon as the mother is recognised to be a separate individual she is experienced as free to enter relationships with others. The prototype of these others is the father participating in an imagined or real sexual relationship, and the reality of the mother's freedom to love others is classically epitomised by the birth of a sibling. Sometimes even the freedom and independence of the mother is provocative when she is observed to have a relationship with her own thoughts.

Although the pain and frustration of waiting for the mother to return is an immediate consequence of disillusion, a different order of time arises when the child realises that he has to wait to grow up before he can do grown-up things and bridge the gap between infancy and adulthood. It is, however, the creativity of the parental couple that may produce the most acute difficulty not least because it provokes envy.

Money-Kyrle's formulation suggests that it is the parents' intercourse that is viewed as the supremely creative act but a brief reflection shows that, while the act of intercourse is essential for creativity, it is far from sufficient. For a creative outcome to be fruitful the brief and often inglorious act of coupling has to be followed by the provision of a suitable setting within which a child can develop and mature. The importance of time is clear when we consider that nine months of pregnancy followed by a prolonged period of care during an extended childhood are required for the creative act to bear fruit, and the same is true of the symbolic creativity in other areas where an inspirational idea may be quick but has to be worked over, developed, and published for it to bear fruit.

Nevertheless it is the feeling of being excluded from the parental couple that increases the pain of generational difference and also brings the child up against the appreciation of a difference between the sexes. In fact gender differences only became substantial after the expulsion from Eden and it is only after the fall that Adam and Eve are allocated different tasks. In Eden their roles were pretty interchangeable but afterwards real gender differences emerged and can be recognised to be essential for creativity. Mitchell, (2013) has suggested that it is with the birth of a real or imagined sibling that questions of creativity and gender begin to be appreciated as we articulate the critical questions of: "Where do babies come from?" and "Will it be a girl or a boy?"

The third fact: the recognition of the inevitability of time and ultimately death

Eventually an awareness of time extends to the experience of waiting for ageing and death which is so often "forced on us, much against our will" (Money-Kyrle, 1971, p. 443). It begins with the awareness that good experiences do not go on forever, and that the same is true of life itself. The passage of time seems to be difficult for all of us to accept and even those who do not believe in an afterlife frequently deny the finality of death and gain comfort from illusions of immortality.

In a broader sense the Garden of Eden Illusion protects us from the recognition of suffering in general and from an awareness that bad things happen and bad people exist. The illusion reveals itself to be a widespread unconscious belief when we ask why suffering is necessary in what ought to be a better world. An awareness of suffering is one of the ways reality makes itself felt as the child interacts with a world which inflicts such unaccountable traumas. Attacks from persecutors can arouse fight and flight reactions but confrontations with deprivation, illness and death also invite feelings of guilt which can weaken our self-confidence and make us aware of the existence of destructiveness within ourselves. Phantasies of our own hurtful attacks on our good objects based on envy, jealousy and greed are inevitably part of our response to the world and make up some of the least palatable of the facts of life. They raise questions about the place of evil in the world, and suggests that facing the reality of death also involves facing the reality of destructive impulses from within. Man's disobedience "brought death into the world with all its woes", and it also brought envy, destructiveness and guilt, that were previously denied or split off into Satan's domain. Milton explains that after his fall Lucifer's name has been changed to Satan since he is no longer the bringer of light but the harbinger of evil.

Perverse scenarios and part-object relationships

Perhaps the most important misrepresentation of reality occurs when personal relationships, particularly that between the frustrated infant and his mother are stripped of their human characteristics and treated as part-objects. The relationship between people is then perverted into one between anatomical elements and this allows them to be mistreated without a full awareness of the suffering involved. Indeed many of the primitive phantasies that deal with humiliation by inflicting it on others are striking in the cruelty of the sadism involved. Hatred and a wish for revenge are expressed in part-object terms involving bottoms, breasts, mouths, vaginas, and penises often in receipt of cruel punishments and mutilations. They commonly involve body parts that are divorced from any connection with a human being and this means that the cruelty can be repeated endlessly without seeming to have any human consequences. Stoller (1975) puts this point when he writes:

> Perversion emphasizes anatomical more than interpersonal gratification. To need to reduce another person to a breast or a penis or a bit of cloth before one can succeed in concentrating one's lust is very sad—and dangerous; such severe failure of potency and degradation of lovingness only augment the other processes that today disintegrate one's humanity.
>
> Stoller (1975, pp. 64–91)

These anatomical representations of relationships are also general rather than personal as if they refer to any mouth in relation to any breast and in that way may connect with primal phantasies that evolved before a personal relationship had been established. The erotisation of the interaction can increase the sadism by adding sexual excitement while avoiding the restraints that would arise if the personal hurt was being recognised.

Misconceptions of the first fact of life: narcissistic perversions

In relation to the first fact of life, namely the dependence on a good external object, Money-Kyrle describes how misconceptions may make use of "a *spuriously satisfying substitute*" for the good object. This spurious object may either be idealised and identified with, or denigrated, controlled, and attacked. The infant may find a more benign replacement for the breast in the form of his thumb or a dummy but when this eventually fails to satisfy the frustration turns to revenge and satisfaction is sought through perverse phantasies.

Money-Kyrle uses material from Meltzer's paper on anal masturbation (1966) to illustrate how, in phantasy, the infant's own bottom can become a spurious substitute for the maternal breast and then become the primary focus of phantasies. While waiting for the nipple to be offered, the infant deals with his frustration by misrepresenting the breast as his own bottom, where the nipple has been replaced by an opening, through which the substitute breast can be entered and controlled. Through this type of phantasy the idealisation is transferred from the supremely satisfying breast to a perversely satisfying bottom. Sometimes the bottom is idealised but when humiliation is prominent the bottom becomes the focus of punishment and humiliation that is intended for the breast.

Misrepresentations of the second fact of live: oedipal perversions

The primal scene is also most commonly misrepresented through a variety of narcissistic identifications leading to phantasies that transform the feeling of exclusion from the parental couple into one of participation. Again, the phantasy of the child and one parent making up an idealised exclusive couple can lead to romantic daydreams from which the other parent and siblings are excluded. However, when participation in the ideal couple fails to be satisfying, the intercourse may be misrepresented as a sadistic relationship which the child may excitedly enter as a participant in sadomasochistic phantasies and daydreams.

In these scenarios the patient identifies with one parent while the other is excluded and placed in the humiliating position which the child had previously occupied, feeling left out, small, and envious. Sometimes this is played out in the transference when the analyst is obliged to watch the spuriously created pair in their idealised coupling (Steiner, 2008).

When the idealisation fails misrepresentations and bottom–breast confusions can lead to scenes of cruelty and humiliation including the sadistic pornography related to beating phantasies such as those which interested and puzzled Freud (1919). Both the patient himself, an imagined sibling, or his mother can be punished in these scenarios involving cruelty and degradation which arise from distortions of both the parents' relationship with the child and with each other. The excitement associated with sexual perversions may give them an addictive hold on the personality and the patient may feel himself to be imprisoned in a destructive world such as that ruled by Satan in his dedication to hatred and revenge (Steiner, 2013).

Misrepresentations of the third fact of life: the erotising of libidinal narcissism

As we have seen, time makes itself felt in the first two facts of life but it makes a direct impact in its own right when it is recognised to be unstoppable, unidirectional, and irreversible. Romantic daydreams may then evolve using scenarios which elicit admiration in order to regain a position of superiority. Usually these involve erotised scenes in which ideal solutions are created and these frequently lead to feelings of triumph over less favoured rivals. Similar phantasies sometimes involving sporting or military triumphs are also commonly used to deal with feelings of exclusion and inferiority. As described in Chapter 1, the timelessness of the romantic world means that, in contrast to more explicit pornography, desire is rarely consummated and pleasure is obtained from endless anticipation, endlessly repeating the moment just before the lovers are about to kiss. Often the pleasure is derived from the triumph over a rival who is imagined to be watching.

At other times the idealisation has moral overtones and nearly all religions speak of an afterlife, sometimes like Milton specifically anticipating a return to the Garden of Eden, "to regain the blissful seat". Such beliefs provide comfort for many people and non-religious versions commonly involve political utopias in which losses are reversed in phantasies of a perfect future.

The capacity to survive disillusionment, to accept reality and to release the capacity to love

If the trauma of disillusion can be tolerated a new relationship that accepts reality can develop and open the door to long-term advantages. These however only become apparent over time and they are not available to the patient at the moment of crisis when he has to suffer the feeling of humiliation that demand such immediate relief. It is therefore vital for the analyst to support the patient to endure and survive rather than evade humiliation and to do this the analyst himself has to be able to tolerate the passage of time and not to expect immediate results.

In Chapter 1 I described how normally, the mother's love helps the dethroned infant to survive because it creates a link and is felt to rescue the baby from the abyss (Sodre, 2012). In favourable circumstances a caring mother is able to help the infant to recover from the disillusionment by showing him that he can still be loved, and that there is sufficient love available for him to get his share amid his rivals in the family. This means that some of the nastiness of humiliation both received by the infant and meted out by him to others needs to be accepted and recognised as inevitable and to some degree accommodated to. Of course this is not always possible but when it does at least in part take place the recognition of difference can be used to establish a feeling of independence and separateness between the self and the object. The object may then be seen more realistically and when it is no longer an idealised possession, a more realistic place in the family can develop.

The working through of feelings of disillusion requires that both the loss of the ideal and the loss of omnipotence associated with it is accepted and mourned. In the absence of time, mourning and loss do not become part of everyday life and this means that in Paradise, love is superficial since it is based on libidinal feelings alone. Love acquires a new depth when we become aware of the sorrow we feel when we hurt our good objects. As splitting lessens the self becomes enlarged and more integrated since both love and hate are recognised as belonging to the self. If negative feelings fail to emerge, then the deeper feelings of love also fail to emerge. These considerations help us to understand why some patients may find love too painful and will try to avoid and deflect loving feelings, sometimes by increasing hatred and grievance.

Nevertheless the recognition of hatred can deepen feelings of love that emerge as regret, guilt, and the wish to make reparation become accessible. The romantic love of the Garden of Eden Illusion then seems to be superficial and based on libidinal feelings alone while the more enduring mature love that follows suffering retains its undertones of ambivalence but feels deeper and more enduring.

Notes

1 Based on Steiner, J. (2018) Overcoming Obstacles in Analysis: Is It Possible to Relinquish Omnipotence and Accept Receptive Femininity? *Psychoanalytic Quarterly*, 87, 1–20, and Steiner, J. (2018a) Time and the Garden of Eden Illusion. *International Journal of Psychoanalysis*, 99, 1274–1287.
2 Elsewhere I have described feelings along a spectrum of embarrassment, shame and humiliation. Even though the discomfort increases at the humiliation end of the spectrum all these feelings demand immediate relief and phrases such as "I wish the ground would open up so I could disappear" seem to apply even what seems like relatively mild embarrassment. The unbearabiltiy of humiliation seems to be increased by the feeling that it is mediated through the agency of a super figure.

6   The unbearability of being feminine[1]

The universal propensity to treat women as inferior has lessened over the years as the rights of women have become recognised and the prejudice against them has been exposed. Nevertheless the tendency to denigrate femininity and to idealise a phallic masculinity perseveres despite social and political change, probably because it is deeply affected by unconscious anxieties which remain poorly understood. There seems to be something unbearable about being feminine which pressures both men and women to idealise masculine qualities and to undervalue feminine ones. While there are many possible factors involved I will suggest in this chapter that our early dependence on feminine qualities in the mother leads first to an idealisation of feminine goodness and then to an envious denigration. Because both female and male elements are required to enable creative developments to take place the idealisation of phallic power with its hatred of femininity is particularly likely to create obstacles in development and to prevent progress in analysis.

The treasure and vulnerability of the feminine

In a passage from Daniel Deronda George Eliot wrote of the value of women in the following terms:

> In these delicate vessels is borne onward through the ages the treasure of human affection.
>
> (George Eliot, 1876, Chapter 11, p. 160)[2]

Eliot sees women as valuable because through their capacity to love and care they become symbols of human goodness. She added that once they are seen as valuable they are fought over by men:

> They are the Yea or Nay of that good for which men are enduring and fighting.
>
> (George Eliot, 1876, Chapter 11, p. 160)

The fact that women are described as vessels implies that they have a three-dimensional interior into which contents can be inserted and removed, and they are seen as delicate, emphasising the vulnerability of the feminine. All these qualities reappear in Klein's writing about women which helps to establish femininity as a symbol of an enduring kind of love. While Money-Kyrle could propose that the parents' intercourse was symbolic of a "supremely creative act", this act is rather short-lived and is often neither glorious nor loving. However it is the feminine capacity to love, of course manifest in the care from both parents, that extends through the time of gestation to the long period of dependence of the human infant that allows the fruit of creation to develop and grow. It represents an extension over time that contrasts with the immediacy of gratification offered by phallic power. However the value of femininity is rarely recognised and I suggest that this is because it is first idealised and then denigrated to fend off the envy that becomes such a problem in relation to good objects. In my discussion of Freud's widely misunderstood thesis on the repudiation of femininity I suggest that it is envy that lies at the root of our inability to tolerate it, leading to the tendency of both men and women to disparage and repudiate femininity and to idealise masculinity in its place.

The appearance of gender differences

As development proceeds, reality makes an impact in a variety of ways some of which seem particularly difficult to accept and give rise to deeply held resistances. It comes as something of a shock to recognise that gender differences stand out as particularly problematic aspects of reality. In Freud's descriptions of the evolution of the fetish described in Chapter 5, he put forward the view that we begin with a deeply held denial of gender difference in which the mother is believed to possess a penis just as the father does. When observations contradict this belief and reality can no longer be ignored, a compromise evolves in which the original belief and the objective observation are able to co-exist. This enables femininity to be repudiated and women to be treated as fetish-objects that can be both possessed and denigrated.

I will argue that such attitudes misrepresent femininity and lead to major obstacles to progress in analysis. Freud described how in women this repudiation is expressed as penis envy, "a positive striving to possess a male genital" while in the male it emerges as "a struggle against his passive or feminine attitude to another male". In this chapter I will develop the view that, in both sexes, what Freud was describing was a preference for phallic masculinity and a denigration of femininity. It is puzzling to consider why it is that femininity is so commonly viewed as shameful and inferior. One factor may be linked to the vulnerability of the feminine and Freud asserts that the repudiation in both sexes is a response to the castration complex, which arises with the discovery of gender differences. He described how the recognition that the woman does not have a penis gives rise to a fear of attack and genital mutilation accompanied by a phantasy that women have already been castrated and are consequently viewed as inferior and defined in terms of a lack. I believe that in both men and women these attitudes are common and represent a major distortion of the facts of life that is based on an overvaluation of the phallus as an attempt to deny the true value and vulnerability of the feminine.

Gender differences play a critical part in the sense of identity and influence one's place in the family hierarchy, irrespective of actual capabilities and strengths. Of course one's place in the great chain of being is historically established on the basis of physical power and the ability to coerce a weaker member. A measure of mastery is readily provided by the ability to humiliate, and the ability to threaten castration can come to symbolise relative power.

These common prejudices attack the true value of the feminine and unless acknowledged, relinquished, and atoned for, they profoundly affect mental development. Femininity, especially because it is associated with receptivity is essential for the establishment of creative relationships and when it is repudiated in favour of phallic superiority development suffers. It is therefore perhaps less surprising than it initially seems, that Freud discusses it in "Analysis Terminable and Interminable" (1937), as a critical factor creating obstacles to progress in analysis. Indeed he was so convinced of the importance of this factor that he described its existence as a bedrock beyond which progress becomes impossible.

Obstacles to progress in analysis

Every practising psychoanalyst is familiar with analyses that become stuck in an atmosphere that feels repetitive and stultifying. At times it seems as if the treatment has come up against a barrier beyond which it is impossible to proceed, and this presents a difficult situation for both the patient and the analyst. Should they tolerate the frustration to see if something new can develop? That could lead to interminable analysis. Or should they accept the limitations and allow the analysis to end? On a larger scale, the same dilemma faces our theoretical understanding of obstacles in general. Sometimes obstacles can act as a stimulus to a theoretical advance which may lead to a better understanding and enable progress to be resumed. At other times, a better theoretical understanding can help us to accept limitations on what analysis can achieve.

Freud's pessimism: "thus our activities are at an end"

This dilemma is the theme of Freud's famous late treatise, "Analysis Terminable and Interminable" (1937), in which he examines obstacles to change and concludes that they often involve physiological and biological factors not susceptible to analytic work. Having concluded that ultimately, "our activities are at an end" he attributed the limitation to two factors, namely the operation of the *death instinct* on the one hand and to the *repudiation of femininity* on the other.

In fact the first seven sections of Freud's paper are devoted to various physical and constitutional factors and in Section VII the most important of these obstacles is attributed to the death instinct. He writes:

> No stronger impression arises from the resistances during the work of analysis than of there being a force that is defending itself by every possible means against recovery and which is absolutely resolved to hold on to illness and suffering ...
>
> These phenomena are unmistakable indications of the presence of a power in mental life which we call the instinct of aggression or of destruction according to its aims, and which we trace back to the original death instinct of living matter.
>
> (Freud, 1937, p. 243)

Freud's views with respect to both the death instinct on the one hand and to the repudiation of femininity on the other are controversial and our contemporary approach to them differs significantly from that held 80 years ago when his book was published. In this chapter I am going to attempt to modify rather than to dismiss his views to see if a contemporary Kleinian approach can rescue some of his basic ideas and even perhaps enable new ones to be applied to the problem of resistance. I will first try to avoid some of the controversy over the death instinct by discussing the role of envy which I see as the chief way that the death instinct is expressed. Then I will explain why I think that the repudiation of femininity is a consequence of envious attacks on femininity which is initially idealised and then envied. Finally I will try to show that it is the capacity to be receptive that is a critical element in femininity.

An anti-life instinct expressed as envy

Freud was concerned to link the ultimate cause of resistance in analysis to the operation of a destructive force which he saw as an expression of the death instinct and Klein supported him in this view. The primary conflict of the two fundamental instincts of life and death were connected by her to the expression of love and hate as they arise towards the good object. Envy inevitably arises in conjunction with love as a reaction to the goodness and value of an object. Initially the hatred is kept apart from love as a result of splitting but when integration proceeds the presence of envy ensures that love and hate are directed to the same object.

Klein saw envy as:

> an oral-sadistic and anal-sadistic expression of destructive impulses, operative from the beginning of life, and that it has a constitutional basis
>
> (1957, p. 176)

While there may be disagreement about the importance and nature of the death instinct there does seem to be abundant evidence of a deeply ingrained resistance to change supporting Freud's contention that something in all of us "is defending itself by every possible means against recovery". If we modify the views of both Klein and Freud and replace the idea of a death instinct with that of an anti-life instinct expressed as envy we can postpone an examination of the deeper meaning of these processes and concentrate on the situations that provoke and sustain envy. We can also explore the mechanisms and phantasies through which destructive attacks are mounted, and examine the aftermath of destructive attacks and their effect on the individual and his relationships.

What provokes envy?

It seems to me possible that the persistent and habitual denigration of femininity that we see both culturally and in analysis is in fact based on an earlier and perhaps deeper appreciation of femininity which is valued and indeed overvalued and idealised. Klein argued that a good relation with the breast as a symbol of maternal value was vital if the infant was to establish good internal object relationships in order to provide the foundation for future development (Klein, 1957). She wrote:

> We find in the analysis of our patients that the breast in its good aspect is the prototype of maternal goodness, inexhaustible patience and generosity, as well as of creativeness. It is these phantasies and instinctual needs that so enrich the primal object that it remains the foundation for hope, trust and belief in goodness.
>
> (Klein, 1957, p. 180)

However, she also recognised that envy led to a hatred, initially focused on the mother and her breast, but subsequently directed against any relationship made by the mother which threatens to intrude and disturb the perfection of the primal couple. What seemed especially likely to provoke envy were images of the mother's rich potential to relate both to external figures in the family and to her internal world. For example,

> the mother receiving the father's penis, having babies inside her, giving birth to them, and being able to feed them.
>
> (Klein, 1957, p. 183)

Envy is then often experienced in response to signs of the mother being an independent person, engaged with others or even with her own thoughts—her mind seemingly turned away from her infant to her internal objects, including her husband and her unborn babies. These images represent the mother as a participant in generative couple, with her baby in the early oral relationship and with her husband in a primal scene, and they all provoke envy. Especially when we feel excluded we envy what we most value and here what is attacked are all those activities that symbolise growth, development, liveliness and creativity, both in the creation of new life and in caring for it, sustaining it and protecting it.

At a part object level the creative symbol may involve the link between nipple and mouth, and between penis and vagina, but these symbols can be extended to areas beyond the concrete level to include mental functions such as feeling and thinking. Hence in his description of "attacks on linking" Bion suggested that envious attacks are directed towards:

> anything which is felt to have the function of linking one object with another
>
> (Bion, 1959, p. 308)

Here Bion includes the link between the analyst's verbal thought offered to the mind of the patient, where both the receptive capacity of the patient's mind and the ideas offered by the analyst can become the focus of envious attacks on the link between them. Feldman (2000), has argued that all such life-affirming activities become the focus of anti-life attacks closely related to envy, and that there is no need to go beyond this to postulate a death seeking instinct.

Envy and the repudiation of femininity

Envious attacks can succeed in destroying the creative link by a focus on either the male or the female component of the couple, but it does seem that images that involve the feminine receptive component of the link are particularly valued and particularly provocative of hatred. It is not clear why this should be so or even if it only appears to be so because envy of true creative masculinity may be hidden beneath a desire for phallic omnipotence which is perhaps itself an envious attack. Nevertheless with her capacity for fecundity on the one hand, for her role in the care and feeding of the infant, and perhaps in part because of her vulnerability, it is the woman, particularly her breast and her genitals, that so often seem to bear the brunt of attacks; in my view, it is this which leads to the repudiation of femininity in favour of a phallic masculinity. These considerations allow us to look at Section VIII of "Analysis Terminable and Interminable" from a new point of view and to see Freud's observations as arising from his patients' unconscious phantasies rather than as a description of normal female development (Britton, 2003).

Freud introduces the repudiation of femininity as a novel theme quite unconnected with the rest of the book and I have found it remarkably easy for the reader, including myself, to overlook it. Thompson (1991), in his detailed analysis of the paper heads his discussion of Section VIII as "The Surprising Turn" and states that,

> It seems curious that this factor, after the careful arguments about the limitations on psychoanalytic treatment that precede its introduction, is declared to be the "bedrock" of resistance to progress.
>
> (Thompson, 1991, p. 175)

Freud's critical paragraphs read as follows:

> Both in therapeutic and in character-analyses we notice that two themes come into especial prominence and give the analyst an unusual amount of trouble. It soon becomes evident that a general principle is at work here. ... The two corresponding themes are, in the female, an envy for the penis—a positive striving to possess a male genital—and, in the male, a struggle against his passive or feminine attitude to another male. What is common to the two themes was singled out at an early date by psychoanalytic nomenclature as an attitude towards the castration complex.
>
> (Freud, 1937, p. 250)

Freud believed that both of these factors led to an unyielding resistance.

> The decisive thing remains that the resistance prevents any change from taking place—that everything stays as it was. We often have the impression that with the wish for a penis and the masculine protest we have penetrated through all the psychological strata and have reached bedrock, and that thus our activities are at an end. This is probably true, since for the psychic field the biological field does play the part of the underlying bedrock. The repudiation of femininity can be nothing else than a biological fact, a part of the great riddle of sex. It would be hard to say whether and when we have succeeded in mastering this factor in an analytic treatment.
>
> (Freud, 1937, pp. 252–253)

These two paragraphs, and the male superiority that they imply, today seem anachronistic and prejudiced. The idea of the woman as inferior, passive, and characterised by lack, has been vigorously challenged, early on by Horney (1924, 1926), Riviere (1929), and Deutsch (1925), and more recently by a large number of writers including Chasseguet-Smirgel (1976), and Birksted-Breen (1993, 1996). These together with an extensive feminist literature (Person and Ovesey, 1983, Dimen, 1997, Goldner, 2000, Balsam, 2013) mean that we no longer think of feminine inferiority as a fact. Britton (2003) suggested that Freud's picture of a woman who *lacks* everything is a defence to counter an image of the mother as the woman who *has* everything. In this respect Klein's work has been a major impetus to revisions of Freud's picture of feminine inferiority, common in his time and still common in the form of sexist prejudice.

Redefining the creative link

Both the male and the female components of the creative link are misrepresented in Freud's claim that the problem arises because of,

> in the female, an envy for the penis—a positive striving to possess a male genital—and, in the male, a struggle against his passive or feminine attitude to another male.

First I will argue that the "positive striving to possess a male genital" in this situation is more appropriately thought of as a wish to possess omnipotent phallic superiority and is a desire prevalent in both men and women as a defence against dependency and need. Second I will suggest that there is nothing passive or inferior about femininity and that Freud's view of a "struggle against a passive or feminine attitude" is in fact a struggle against the adoption of a receptive position, which although feminine in its imagery, is equally important for both men and women to accept. Both men and women have to be able to adopt a receptive stance, not only in relation to the breast in infancy, but also in order to be receptive to the thoughts and feelings of others through a capacity to receive and contain projections. However this should not be taken to mean that there are no differences between the way men and women react. It is rather that in the area of obstacles to progress they have many issues in common and all of us have to be able to accept the existence of both male and female phantasies and to tolerate the link between them.

The resistance to progress delineated by Freud can thus be thought to arise from the predilection to phallic omnipotence on the one hand and from the reluctance to adopt a receptive position on the other. Here the nipple, the penis, and the analyst's thoughts can be viewed as "entering", "inserting", or "giving", while the mouth, vagina, and the patient's mind are "receiving". However the traffic goes both ways and just as the mother must be open to the projections of her baby it is essential for the analyst to be receptive to the projections of the patient if a creative relationship is to be established.

It seems to me that receptivity is a capacity that leads to some of the most important and valued qualities that we associate with femininity in both men and women. These include creativity and the capacity to engage with an internal world associated with images of pregnancy and care for others. It is an essential stance for us to be able to adopt if we wish to give and receive from others and thereby to grow and to develop both in life and in analysis.

For progress in analysis to be resumed following a setback both the male and female elements need to be restored to their true value so that a receptive femininity can join with a benign masculinity in a functional creative link—namely a link in which omnipotence is relinquished and feminine receptiveness is valued and accepted. We can surely agree with Freud that this task is difficult, but the redefinition I have attempted allows us to explore each of these elements in turn and to examine if further understanding can restore progress or if it forces us, at least temporarily, to accept the existence of a bedrock.

Phallic omnipotence and narcissistic organisations

The idea that the *penis envy* referred to by Freud may more appropriately be thought of as *phallus envy* or even perhaps as *omnipotence envy, is* in keeping with the views of Birksted-Breen who proposed that,

> Penis envy is often phallus envy, the wish to have or be the phallus which, it is believed, will keep at bay feelings of inadequacy, lack, and vulnerability.

(Birksted-Breen, 1996, p. 651)

She contrasted phallic masculinity, which is based on omnipotence and a desire to control and dominate objects with a masculinity that recognises relationships and values femininity, which she called "penis as link". It is the omnipotent version of masculinity that is turned to as a defence and which is often also the vehicle for destructive envious attacks against creative links.

While the imagery of the phallus is masculine, the desire for omnipotence arises in both male and female patients and both commonly turn to phallic phantasies to magically solve the pains of reality. Indeed creative links are often envied and hated precisely because they involve the capacity to tolerate the lack of omnipotence.

The most common manifestation of omnipotent phallic phantasies takes the form of narcissistic idealisations based on pathological organisations which create a powerful image of phallic superiority as a defence against dependence, vulnerability, and need (Rosenfeld, 1971, Steiner, 1993). They commonly create illusions of idealised states based on omnipotent control of ideal objects, which are sometimes believed to have existed in reality rather than in phantasy, often in the form of a blissful Paradise at the breast or sometimes even in the womb. As discussed in Chapter 1, these Garden of Eden Illusions underpin the omnipotent phantasies described by Akhtar (1996) that "someday" the bliss will be magically restored or alternatively that they might still exist "if only" the disaster had been avoided.

When the idealisation collapses the patient may respond with a terrible sense of disillusionment sometimes felt as a catastrophe and often

associated with feelings of having been robbed or even castrated. It was perhaps such phantasies that led Freud to his image of woman as a castrated
man even though it seems to me to be clear that such fears are based on
the collapse of defensive phantasies and affect both male and female
patients.

The relinquishment of omnipotence

It might be thought that the giving up of omnipotence and accepting receptive femininity would yield its own rewards but such benefits tend to be
delayed and uncertain. By contrast omnipotence works instantly and with
a magical certainty and often seems to have such a hold on the personality
that its relinquishment is problematic. Freud claimed that it is never possible to fully give up a source of instinctual satisfaction (Freud, 1908,
p. 145), and it is probably never possible to fully relinquish the pleasures of
omnipotence. Perhaps as Freud suggests the best we can do is to acknowledge its existence, to recognise the damage it can do, and to watch if its
hold on the personality can weaken. To do this we must admit the pleasure
that omnipotent destructive phantasies provide, so that the omnipotence
can be properly missed and mourned (Segal, 1994). However even when
phallic omnipotence is to some extent replaced by the idea of a "penis as
link", a second task confronts the patient which may be equally difficult,
and this involves the acceptance of a receptive femininity in order to permit
the restoration of a creative couple.

Phantasies of feminine mutilation

We then have to consider why it is that femininity is so difficult to value
and accept and it is here that unconscious phantasies of female mutilation
may play a part. These phantasies lead to receptivity being associated with
images of the female genital that is not only vulnerable, but is felt to be
inferior, repellent, and even disgusting. To understand how these images
arise I believe it is necessary to recognise that some of the primitive unconscious phantasies that make up the aftermath of destructive attacks may be
extremely disturbing and provoke aversion.

   Klein for example described how violent some of the unconscious phantasies can be.

> In his destructive phantasies he bites and tears up the breast, devours
> it, annihilates it; and he feels that the breast will attack him in the same
> way. As urethral and anal-sadistic impulses gain in strength, the infant
> in his mind attacks the breast with poisonous urine and explosive
> faeces, and therefore expects it to be poisonous and explosive
> towards him.
>
> (Klein, 1957, p. 63)

Sometimes the nipple is the focus of hatred when it is associated with a masculine aspect of the mother, which is seen as hostile to the infant and protecting the mother by limiting access to the breast. Biting off the nipple may give rise to an image of the breast as damaged, bleeding and mutilated and may form the basis for phantasies of the female genital as castrated, damaged, and vulnerable to hostile intrusions.

Riviere described how the sadism comes to be directed towards the mother's body.

> The desire to bite off the nipple shifts, and desires to destroy, penetrate and disembowel the mother and devour her and the contents of her body, succeed it. These contents include the father's penis, her fæces and her children—all her possessions and love-objects, imagined as within her body. The desire to bite off the nipple is also shifted, as we know, on to the desire to castrate the father by biting off his penis. Both parents are rivals in this stage, both possess desired objects; the sadism is directed against both and the revenge of both is feared.
>
> (Riviere, 1929, p. 309)

Klein describes further details of how violent, disturbing, and primitive the phantasies may become.

> The phantasied onslaughts on the mother follow two main lines: one is the predominantly oral impulse to suck dry, bite up, scoop out and rob the mother's body of its good contents. ... The other line of attack derives from the anal and urethral impulses and implies expelling dangerous substances (excrements) out of the self and into the mother. ... These excrements and bad parts of the self are meant not only to injure but also to control and to take possession of the object.
>
> (Klein, 1957, p. 63)

Sometimes a vertical split may appear in which feelings of repulsion are directed towards the lower half of the body and especially to the female genital. We see this in Shakespeare's Lear whose hatred for his daughters is expressed through his disgust.

> But to the girdle do the gods inherit; beneath is all the fiends'. There's hell, there's darkness, there's the sulfurous pit—burning, scalding, stench, consumption! Fie, fie, fie, pah, pah!—Give me an ounce of civet, good apothecary, to sweeten my imagination. There's money for thee.
>
> (King Lear, Act 4. Scene 6)

Freud (1930) pursued this theme when he linked the development of feelings of disgust to the time in prehistory when man assumed an erect posture.

Standing upright led to an enormous expansion in the role of vision and the development of disgust evolved in relation to smell, touch and taste especially towards ano-genital functions. When the female genital becomes the focus of envious anal and urethral attacks it leaves behind a kind of battle scene of mutilated and defiled body parts, so that being feminine and receptive became associated with feelings of vulnerability to phallic attacks combined with repellent images of mutilation and contamination with faeces and urine.

It seems to me that these images associated with sadistic attacks directed at receptive femininity give rise to the preference for the excitements of phallic triumph as well as to feelings of revulsion towards feminine receptivity. The images are frightening and sometimes repulsive and make the task of restoring femininity to its true value a difficult one. Since they are deeply rooted in our unconscious they can only be partially altered by education and social change. We can however hope that a psychoanalytic approach might be more effective and that the analysis of the damage done through envious attacks can set a more benevolent reparative process in motion. If feelings of guilt, regret, and remorse can be tolerated mourning the loss of omnipotence may lead to a less destructive view of masculinity and a less damaged view of receptive femininity.

Receptivity and thinking

Receptive femininity is also vital in the field of ideas where both giving and receiving are necessary in order to think creatively, and sometimes patients seem especially to repudiate female types of thinking and in particular fail to allow the feminine to interact with masculine thinking in a productive way. This is true of the patient I am going to discuss whose analysis became stuck and unproductive because she seemed unable to use her considerable intelligence.

A similar problem in thinking associated with receptive femininity was described by Riviere (1929) in the analysis of a woman of ability and competence who had problems deploying her intelligence. She hid her considerable knowledge and showed deference to men by giving an impression that she was stupid, while seeing through them in an apparently innocent and artless manner. She used a flirtatiousness to conceal an intense rivalry with men and could not accept a deeper view of femininity as receptive, creative, and valuable. Britton also illustrates this theme in a patient who had idealised her analyst as a source of magical power without which she was unable to think. An omnipotent phallus was felt to be a shared possession as long as the phantasy of a mutual idealisation was sustained and exchanges between the analyst and his patient were viewed as a symbolic intercourse. However, neither his patient nor the one described by Riviere, were able to sustain the illusion and its collapse resulted in what a appeared as kind of stupidity.

When this illusion collapses there is not a sense of loss but the phantasy of having been literally or symbolically "castrated". If the phallus is symbolically equated with the intellect the consequent feeling of castration is experienced as losing all mental potency, of being stupid.

(Britton, 2003, p. 66)

Britton described how the loss of the belief in a secret phallic supremacy exposed his patient to the most intense experiences of envy, and despair, and made her feel that she had become mentally defective.

Clinical material, Mrs A

I will present a fragment from the analysis of a patient, Mrs A, who felt blocked in her life and also in her analysis. She complained of feeling trapped and disadvantaged in part because she was a single mother. She admired those people, especially men, who were free to exercise their power and also those women who could live a life of luxury under the protection of powerful men. She seemed to view intelligence as something masculine and powerful but dangerous and damaging both to women and to other men. This led her to repudiate her own intelligence using it mostly to protect herself from intrusive exploitation and in particular she felt she needed to avoid a receptive thoughtfulness in relation to my work.

She emphasised her dissatisfactions stressing the things she lacked, such as a professional career, a husband, and the wealth and comfort that only men could provide. It was striking that she was unable to get pleasure from the good things she did have, like her friends, her work, her children, and especially her capacity to think. She described her work as a futile place with no prospects and no future, and she saw herself as plagued by bad luck and by repeated misfortunes and betrayals. She had no serious relationship and she used her women friends to complain about men and her analysis to reiterate her unhappiness because of the unfair hardships she had to endure.

She described similar resentments towards her father, a lay preacher who had introduced a strict and arbitrary morality into the home, which her mother and her considerably older sister accepted without protest but which she suspected was corrupt and hypocritical. The parents slept in separate rooms and she shared her mother's bed until she was given her own room when she was 8-years-old. She linked many of the feelings of unfairness to this expulsion and she seems never again to have felt loved and valued.

Unlike her sister, who did not go to university but married a successful businessman, she did well at school and earned a place at university where she surprised everyone when she came top of her year in maths and physics. However, in her second year she had a breakdown and was sent home in an acute anxiety state with depersonalisation and some persecutory thoughts. She gradually improved but could not return to college, and after two years she took a secretarial course and worked in a large firm of solicitors eventually rising to a senior and highly responsible position in her office.

When she began analysis she spent many sessions in a rambling, dreamy state, describing her failures and seeming to expect them to be put right for her. She adopted a little-girl quality in her relationships, which were highly erotised and accompanied by a naivety and apparent innocence. She dressed seductively and encouraged men to make advances in a way that tended to put them in the wrong. For example, she held hands under the table with one of the senior lawyers at an office party but expressed outrage when he offered to see her home. In the sessions she was seductive but also easily felt misused and became indignant if I interpreted the erotised atmosphere that she created. It seemed to me that she went into a kind of dream state in which she felt close to me in a vaguely erotised way, but that if this was interpreted the spell was broken and she felt expelled from this intimacy, as she had been from her mother's bed.

One of the most striking aspects of Mrs A's behaviour in her sessions was what I came to think of as her pseudo-imbecility. She would adopt a kind of thoughtless whining and gave the impression that she was unable to think intelligently. For example she would moan, "Why don't you tell me what to do?" or "You didn't tell me I should free-associate. I have been coming all these years and I never knew what I was supposed to do". It was difficult to believe that this same person could have excelled in science at the university, and it was only as I got glimpses of a quite superior intelligence, for example, when she mastered complex and subtle problems at work, or when she pointed out errors of thinking on my part, that I began to realise that she was not properly utilising her capacity to think. In part, she seemed to split it off and project it into me so that she came to depend on me for the most elementary thought, while at the same time she watched me carefully and used her intelligence to point out my errors both factual and ethical. She seemed to view thinking as a masculine activity of a dangerous kind that could be used to exploit and misuse the vulnerability of women. Feminine desire was also dangerous because, in her view, the link between a man and a woman was damaging and exploitative.

A fragment of a session

Here is a fragment of a session in which she began, five minutes late, by explaining that she had been delayed because she had to struggle to get away from a friend who wanted to chat. She then described a dream in which she was descending in the underground but at the foot of the steps found herself having to make a choice between the left-hand passage leading to town and the right-hand one leading to her home. She stood there unable to choose, feeling terribly heavy and found that she had a gardening sickle in her hand. Her indecision made her late and she was relieved since this meant that she did not have time to go into town and could go home and do the work that needed to be done in her garden which was terribly overgrown and untidy. She recalled how often when she felt she had too much work to do she would leave it in a mess and go to town and wander around the shops. A neighbour had loaned the sickle to her some two years previously and she discovered it a few days before while clearing out her garden-shed. She felt guilty, not only because she had not returned it but also because she had never used it. She described it as a horrible sharp thing and wondered why the neighbour had not asked for it back. Perhaps he had forgotten that he had lent it to her.

I interpreted that perhaps the choice that was so heavy in her dream represented the conflict she was in between doing difficult analytic work and fleeing from it. I suggested that she saw her mind as overgrown and untidy like her garden and that there was a lot of work for us to do. Perhaps on her way to the session she had to choose between embarking on this work and chatting with her friend.

In response to these interpretations she said that she felt heavy now and she complained that my interpretations made her feel bad. If there was a lot of work to be done she must still be very ill, and that is a horrible thing to say to a patient. As the session continued she expressed further resentments even though I thought that she had shown a fleeting interest in the dream and my interpretation of it.

Discussion

Mrs A seemed to me to have made some use of the analysis but then became stuck in a situation that, like her work, had become "a futile place". My own disappointment in my work with her led to periods of self-doubt and eventually to the idea that perhaps no further progress was possible and that we may have gone as far as we could go. Gradually I became interested in the question of why we were so stuck and this led me to return to Freud's formulations on the repudiation of femininity as a way of thinking about our situation. I wondered if part of the patient's failure to develop further was connected with the low opinion she had of her femininity on the one hand, together with a fear of using her intelligence on the other. Like Rivière's patient she used her femininity to evoke desire in men, which she then felt obliged to resist because she could not value or feel safe with a receptive femininity.

In her dream she did feel guilty that she had not used the sickle, which she had borrowed and I thought this might point to a capacity to work and to think which she was aware she kept unused. It seemed to me that she did have some idea of a creative femininity but felt obliged to repudiate it, as she did not want to be seen working with me in a cooperative way. If she used her intelligence she would be wielding a sharp and dangerous weapon, an ugly thing. This is how she described my work which she said made her feel bad and she seemed to visualise her own intelligence as having the same destructive dangerous quality.

However in her first year at university she had been able to think and perhaps had allowed herself the freedom to be curious, to reason, and to enjoy her capacities. However this freedom did not last and after her breakdown she was obliged to settle for a secretarial post that she saw as feminine and inferior. Perhaps at that time her freedom to question conventional assumptions were felt to be dangerous if they led her to see through the righteousness of her father's morality. Certainly in the analysis she was quick to see through my own intellectual and ethical shortcomings and then seemed to draw back as if to protect me from a more forceful expression of her views. Sometimes she seemed to be pretending to be stupid so that she could use her intelligence to catch me out and then argue that she could not protect herself because she was a vulnerable woman at the mercy of powerful men. Phantasies of violent mutilation may well have made her expect horrible attacks with sharp sickle-like weapons and made the idea of a receptive femininity repellent and dangerous.

It seemed to me that while feminine receptivity was repudiated so too was a loving and productive masculinity. This meant that she felt she was at the mercy of a phallic superiority and had to protect herself by refusing to let me in. A creative couple in which a receptive feminine side of her could allow a caring side of me to enter became impossible to realise. She claimed that she admired successful men and envied women who did not need to work, but I think she recognised that this view devalued a true feminine creativity, which remained only as a potential within her. Her intense rivalry and jealousy made her fear that if she were to allow a creative intercourse within her mind as well as within the analysis she would become the object of violent envious attacks from others.

Conclusion

As we proceed to study obstacles to progress in development we come up against a variety of factors and in this chapter I have singled out two that are derived from Freud's original observations but are also a significant departure from them. While I have supported the idea that a critical aim is to relinquish idealisation and omnipotence I have argued that both the patient and the analyst have in addition to overcome their reluctance to value femininity and that difficulties arise from either or both of these factors. Omnipotent phallic organisations create idealised retreats which protect the subject from both shame and guilt, and emergence from these states involves both "seeing" and "being seen" (Steiner, 2011). When the attacks are motivated by envy and directed against creative links, the damage to good objects and good relationships may give rise to unbearable feelings of shame and guilt particularly when these are directed at receptive femininity, seen as the weaker and most damaged element of the link.

The analysis has then to provide a supportive structure in which shame and guilt can be examined and the question of whether they are bearable can be explored. Sometimes the patient seems able to accept the loss of phallic superiority and face the guilt of the damage it has done. Moves in this direction are possible if guilt is bearable and when this does prove possible reparative wishes can be mobilised to initiate a benevolent cycle in which objects become less damaged, and less persecutory so that the severity of the super-ego is moderated (Klein, 1957).

However even when moves towards facing these difficult aspects of reality are embarked on, a further difficulty remains if a receptive femininity cannot be accepted and valued. This further step requires the value and importance of receptivity to be acknowledged both within ourselves and in others. The vulnerability associated with opening ourselves to masculine entry requires a vigilance because we can never be sure that the masculinity is not concealing a phallic damaging and exploitative force. Feminine receptivity has to be protected by the creation of a setting in which it is valued and the dangers associated with it are appreciated.

I have described these tasks as if they were problems the patient has to face and as if the analyst functions as a helpful benign influence. It is obvious, however, that the analyst faces precisely the same problems to do with his own omnipotence and precisely the same reluctance to accept his receptive femininity. It is clearly important that the analyst is able to examine his own contribution to the deadlock in the analysis and it is only possible to help the patient with his omnipotence if the analyst has been able to address his own.

Notes

1 Based on Steiner, J. 2018 Overcoming Obstacles in Analysis: Is It Possible to Relinquish Omnipotence and Accept Receptive Femininity? *Psychoanalytic Quarterly*, 87:1–20
2 This passage was made famous when it was misquoted by Henry James who referred to frail vessels rather than delicate ones.

7   The sympathetic imagination

Keats and the movement in and out of projective identification

The response of the analyst to his patient's state of mind is a critical factor in the analysis of Garden of Eden Illusions. We sometimes get drawn into the illusions and partake of a type of *folie à deux*, just as a mother does when she engages in an idealised interaction with her baby. Such engagement creates an empathic sense of understanding in the analyst and a sense of being understood in the patient which is valued by both even though it is based on an illusion that will one day need to be recognised. The recognition of reality can be painful and shocking and takes place when the analyst, or sometimes the patient of course, withdraws from the identification and examines the total situation from the outside. Because of the inevitable trauma reality has to be approached with a sensitive understanding of the pain of disillusion. Consequently we need to be able to engage in the patient's conflicts and also to retain a questioning attitude in which observation of the patient and the task of trying to understand how his mind works is our primary aim.

Normally, we alternate between these two states, emotionally engaged as participants on the one hand and becoming separate to be able to observe on the other, and to achieve this dual role requires a capacity to identify in a flexible and reversible manner. Keeping a proper balance is not always easy, and the analyst may behave inappropriately if he allows himself to get trapped in identifications with his patients or their objects. Equally, he will fail to understand his patient if he behaves only as a detached observer without feeling himself into the patient's experiences. Nevertheless this kind of empathic understanding can be misleading especially when the analyst treats the interpretation as knowledge rather than as a tentative hypothesis. Sometimes we are so sure of what the patient is feeling that we use phrases like "obviously the patient is denying his anger", or "here it is evident that oedipal phantasies are active". It is salutary to observe such certainty in ourselves and to see it as a hallmark of a failure to dis-identify with the patient and observe the total situation from a distance and over time. In this chapter I will explore this capacity to engage through empathy and suggest that it requires a flexible use of projective identification in which we move in and out of identifications.

Understanding via sympathetic intuition

When we enter the patient's mind by projective identification we feel ourselves into his position and observe our own feelings as we intuitively identify with whatever role he is conveying. Of course not all identifications are felt as empathic by the patient. It is the patient's drama we engage with as if we were spectators in a theatre and sometimes we identify and sympathise not with the patient but, for example, with his wife or mother as we hear about their lives. We are nevertheless engaged as a participant in his story, thoughts and feelings are evoked in us and we try to use these feelings to imagine what the patient is experiencing.

Such identifications are initially unconscious and automatic and while they involve projective identification they also require us to be receptive to projections and to allow a free-floating responsiveness of our thoughts and feelings. In this phase of our work we try to engage with an open mind in which we notice what arises within us without directing our thoughts to a specific end. This state of mind is something like that which Bion called maternal reverie, where the critical element is the openness and flexibility in the absence of a fixed focus of attention (Bion, 1962). Free-floating attention is essential if we are to be open to the patient's projections and a free-floating responsiveness is necessary if we are to put ourselves into the patient's situation.

Sympathetic intuition based on projective and introjective identification can give rise to important insights and if it is treated as a provisional hypothesis of what the patient might be feeling it can serve as an essential step towards a more reliable formulation. Of course such inferences may be wrong but no great harm is done if they are recognised as ideas, possibilities or hypotheses, because these can easily be modified and corrected in the subsequent phase of observation.

However, we need to remember that while both patient and analyst use projective identification as a means of communication which is directed to understanding, they also deploy it for a variety of defensive reasons, for example, to disown parts of themselves or to attack and to control their objects (Rosenfeld, 1971; Feldman, 1994; Sodre, 2004). Errors may be more difficult to correct if the inferences are viewed concretely and the more pressure there is in the interaction the more likely it is that the projections become rigid and are tenaciously held onto with an absence of self-doubt.

Sometimes we come to believe that we know what the patient is thinking and feeling and it may then be salutary to heed Adam Smith when he reminds us in a passage written 270 years ago, that we have no direct route to another person's mind.

> As we have no immediate experience of what other men feel, we can form no idea of the manner in which they are affected but by conceiving of what we would feel in a like situation. Though our brother is

upon the rack, as long as we ourselves are at our ease, our senses will never inform us of what he suffers. They never did and never can carry us beyond our persons, and it is by the imagination only that we can form any conception of what are his sensations.

(Smith, 1759)

A similar point is made by Bate (1945, p. 144), in his discussion of romantic literature when he suggests that,

The imagination, by an effort of sympathetic intuition, is able to penetrate the barrier which space puts between it and its object, and, by actually entering into the object, so to speak, secure a momentary but complete identification with it.

Bate uses the term *sympathetic imagination*, introduced by the romantic poets (e.g. Coleridge, 1810; Shelley, 1821) and stresses the "effort of sympathetic intuition" which I have suggested is based on projective and introjective identification. He also points out that the identification must be momentary because, if it is prolonged, it is in danger of changing into an entrenched belief. Here I suggest that once the moment is over, the identification must be withdrawn in order that the patient be observed. Bate describes how empathic projective identification can lead to misattributions and quotes an example from Shakespeare's *King Lear*. The King, still seething from the injustices done to him, meets Poor Tom and in his grief and indignation says, "Didst thou give all to thy daughters, and art thou come to this?" Lear fails to identify empathically with Tom because he assumes that they had identical reasons for their distress. At the same time Shakespeare shows an amazing capacity to put himself into Lear's shoes and to understand his concrete thinking.

Despite its liability to error, *sympathetic imagination* based on projective identification is an essential step in the process of understanding other people, and in analysis it can create a sense of connection in which we suffer with the patient as we temporarily engage with his pleasures and his pains. It is also important as a guide to ethical behaviour as Shelley pointed out when he proposed that it was the "Imagination enlarged by sympathy" that served as "The great instrument of moral good" (1821). This is because it enables us to attribute human feelings to others and treat them as we would like to be treated ourselves. Sympathetic imagination enables feelings of empathy to arise (Beres and Arlow, 1974; Bolognini, 1997) and can affirm a bond of common feeling with others, which is an important aspect of friendship. When it misses the mark, however, it can create resentment and mistrust.

The stage of detached observation

As we withdraw from an identification we relate to the patient from a position of separateness, more fully ourselves as we try to observe the patient as objectively as we can. But observation is also open to errors. Objective facts may themselves become distorted by unconscious processes and these are especially likely to arise if we have failed to empathise, sometimes because of a reluctance to use our imagination or even because of contempt for it. It may then be difficult to imagine what it feels like to be someone who seems different or strange and this can lead to prejudice and cruelty to others. It used to be assumed, for example, that very young infants are not disturbed by pain and until very recently they were commonly operated on without anaesthetic (Coates, 2016). As a young doctor I myself did circumcisions without anaesthetic, blithely failing to observe because I had failed to empathise with the screaming baby. Observation without empathy also led to the assumption that black races did not blush because the redness was not visible. Slave owners took this to mean that they were unable to feel embarrassment or humiliation and could be mistreated with impunity as sub-human.

It is clearly difficult to make judgements about what another person is experiencing and the greater the difference between us the more difficult it is to empathise and observe. Do all living creatures feel pain? Do infants, and animals for that matter, feel envy and jealousy? And to what extent is their experience similar or different from our own. While we can never know what another person feels we are less likely to misunderstand if we combine empathic imagination with objective observation.

The need to move flexibly between identification and observation

Of course, the distinction between the two phases that I have described is schematic and normally there is a constant movement between them. However, this movement can become sluggish and we can become stuck either in a sympathetic over-involvement or in a distant and sometimes judgemental detachment. A balanced view requires us to identify, then to withdraw in order to observe, and then with a modified hypothesis to identify once more in repetitive cycles that hopefully inch towards a greater understanding. Both ways of relating to the patient are essential and complementary and the problem is to find ways to move flexibly and repeatedly between the two. In Chapter 10 I will argue that such flexibility is much easier to sustain if it is accompanied by irony. With irony omnipotence is moderated by self-doubt, disillusion becomes less catastrophic, and a respect for both subjective and objective knowledge can develop (Britton, 2004). However irony is sometimes difficult to achieve especially where emotional pressures lead to concrete thinking with its characteristic rigidity.

It therefore seemed to me important to try to find examples of flexible movement in and out of identification, which we could study and perhaps emulate and I have chosen to look at Keats in his "Ode to a Nightingale".[1] I suspect that poets and artists are especially gifted in this respect and have a capacity both to value their imaginative creations and at the same time to respect the reality of their craft.

Keats and sympathetic imagination

Keats was renowned for his capacity to engage in imaginary flights in which he lost himself in the objects he identified with. He declared that he became "a part of all I see", and stated that, "If a Sparrow comes before my window, I take part in its existence and pick about the gravel". Through such identifications "We may even soar with a hawk, and bend with the movements of a tree in the wind" (Abrams, 1956, p. 74), but I think it is clear that it is not possible to understand what a sparrow feels by this process, to say nothing of a tree in the wind.[2] Through his capacity to identify Keats was discovering things about himself and by describing them helping us to do the same.

The oscillation between the liberating engagement in phantasy and a return to the real world with its limitations and essential isolation and loneliness is marvellously illustrated in the "Ode to a Nightingale".[3] While we can never match his poetic mastery, I believe that we need to discover something similar in our responses to our patients and that it can serve as a model of the conjunction of imagination and observation that we can learn from.

Ode to a Nightingale

The Ode begins in a mood of heaviness and lethargy that contrasts with the freedom of the nightingale (Keats, 1819).

> My heart aches, and a drowsy numbness pains
> My sense, as though of hemlock I had drunk,
> Or emptied some dull opiate to the drains
> One minute past, and Lethe-wards had sunk:

The hemlock has associations to suicide perhaps like that of Socrates based on a refusal to compromise with truth, while the dull opiate and Lethe makes us think of pain-relief, forgetting and oblivion. Keats seems to me to be deeply aware of the pain of living and he is trying to dull that pain, to forget reality and as confirmed later in the poem, even to explore death as a relief from pain.

In an enigmatic comment Keats next denies that his mood arises out of envy.

> Tis not through envy of thy happy lot,
> But being too happy in thine happiness,—
> That thou, light-winged Dryad of the trees
> In some melodious plot
> Of beechen green, and shadows numberless,
> Singest of summer in full-throated ease.

I think Keats knows that he is using his identification with the nightingale to deny reality and to escape from his heart-ache and misery. While envy is alluded to, there is no sign of envious spoiling in the poem perhaps because Keats was transiently able to escape from his depression without losing contact with reality. He does not wallow in his misery and he does not denigrate the object he admires but freely admits that his identification and idealisation is driven by a wish to escape from pain and depression. Moreover even though he claims that he is happy as he imagines the nightingale to be happy, he does not want us to think that the drowsy numbness of the previous stanza has completely left his mind. It remains in our minds too and sets the tone of the poem as one in which we are aware of both the painful state of heart-ache and the blissful state he is trying to reach.

Keats finds that to escape is not as easy as he thought and he begins by turning to wine, first white and then red, as a means of facilitating his flight.

> O, for a draught of vintage! that hath been
> Cool'd a long age in the deep-delved earth,
> Tasting of Flora and the country green,
> Dance, and Provençal song, and sunburnt mirth!
> O for a beaker full of the warm South,
> Full of the true, the blushful Hippocrene,
> With beaded bubbles winking at the brim,
> And purple-stained mouth;
> That I might drink, and leave the world unseen,
> And with thee fade away into the forest dim:

But just as we begin to think that he is enjoying his moment of freedom he reminds us of what he is escaping from.

> Fade far away, dissolve, and quite forget
> What thou among the leaves hast never known,
> The weariness, the fever, and the fret
> Here, where men sit and hear each other groan;
> Where palsy shakes a few, sad, last gray hairs,
> Where youth grows pale, and spectre-thin, and dies;
> Where but to think is to be full of sorrow
> And leaden-eyed despairs,
> Where Beauty cannot keep her lustrous eyes,
> Or new Love pine at them beyond to-morrow.

Here our empathy is deepened by knowledge of the situation Keats was facing at the time of the Odes. His father had died when he was 8 and his mother remarried leaving him in the care of his grandmother. Then when he was 14 his mother died of TB, and, just a few months before he began writing the Ode he nursed his brother Tom who died of the same disease in his rooms in 46 Well Walk in Hampstead. Through his training as an apothecary and dresser at Guy's hospital he had ample opportunity to witness suffering and death, and he was himself to die of TB at the age of 25, less than two years after writing the Ode.

We are not in the same position as Keats but we can imagine what he might be feeling and as we listen to the poetry we can admire his capacity to look at illness and death without flinching. We identify with him and are reminded of our own mortality and our dubious ability to face it. Even as he dwells on the reality of the sorrowful scenes the poetry remains lyrical as if he is ready to rise above it through his verse.

In fact immediately after this section on illness and dying, Keats soars away again, now relying on "the viewless wings of poesy" to persuade the "dull brain" to abandon its adherence to reality.

> Away! away! for I will fly to thee,
> Not charioted by Bacchus and his pards,
> But on the viewless wings of Poesy,
> Though the dull brain perplexes and retards:
> Already with thee! tender is the night,
> And haply the Queen-Moon is on her throne,
> Cluster'd around by all her starry Fays;

It is with relief that we join Keats in the fairy-tale world of tenderness and moonlight but again we are quickly brought back to reality.

> But here there is no light,
> Save what from heaven is with the breezes blown
> Through verdurous glooms and winding mossy ways.
> I cannot see what flowers are at my feet,
> Nor what soft incense hangs upon the boughs,
> But, in embalmed darkness, guess each sweet
> Wherewith the seasonable month endows
> The grass, the thicket, and the fruit-tree wild;
> White hawthorn, and the pastoral eglantine;
> Fast fading violets cover'd up in leaves;
> And mid-May's eldest child,
> The coming musk-rose, full of dewy wine,
> The murmurous haunt of flies on summer eves.

The sadness is both beautiful and moving and we can think of the Queen Moon observing us not from a manic superiority but with a tenderness befitting her understanding of the scene.[4]

In identification with Keats we listen through the gloom and are brought back again to the prospect of dying.

> Darkling I listen; and, for many a time
> I have been half in love with easeful Death,
> Call'd him soft names in many a mused rhyme,
> To take into the air my quiet breath;
> Now more than ever seems it rich to die,
> To cease upon the midnight with no pain,
> While thou art pouring forth thy soul abroad
> In such an ecstasy!
> Still wouldst thou sing, and I have ears in vain—
> To thy high requiem become a sod.

Death is here a relief from pain and its sting is lessened by the phantasy that the nightingale will live on and continue his singing even after the poet is dead. However, once again Keats soars off to identify with the nightingale as a creature who is able to be free because it has no conception of death.

> Thou wast not born for death, immortal Bird!

Keats knows, even though the bird does not, that the nightingale will die like any other living creature. Like the "Fast fading violets" the nightingale too will soon be "cover'd up in leaves", as too will Keats, and as too will the reader however distant the prospect. Nevertheless he tries once more to evade this truth and to imagine a continuity with previous nightingales in times long past.

> Thou wast not born for death, immortal Bird!
> No hungry generations tread thee down;
> The voice I hear this passing night was heard
> In ancient days by emperor and clown:
> Perhaps the self-same song that found a path
> Through the sad heart of Ruth, when, sick for home,
> She stood in tears amid the alien corn;
> The same that oft-times hath
> Charm'd magic casements, opening on the foam
> Of perilous seas, in faery lands forlorn.

Keats seems to me to imply that, like some narcissistically deluded people, the nightingale has illusions of immortality, based on the idea that successive individual nightingales are all represented in the present one. One way of evading death is to believe that our children and our work will survive and support an illusion of immortality. Shakespeare claimed something similar when, I think with irony rather than delusion, he wrote:

> So long as men can breathe or eyes can see,
> So long lives this and this gives life to thee.
>   (Sonnet 18, "Shall I compare thee to
>   a summer's day?")

Both Keats and Shakespeare are using irony to recognise the universal need for illusion as a comfort from the harsh facts imposed by thoughts of the reality of death. Keats allies himself with generations of mortal human beings who, like him, engaged in fairy-tale worlds and were comforted and "charmed" by the song of nightingales.

He is momentarily seduced by this theme but is again brought firmly back to earth when he notices the word *forlorn*.

> Forlorn! the very word is like a bell
> To toll me back from thee to my sole self!
> Adieu! the fancy cannot cheat so well
> As she is fam'd to do, deceiving elf.

He restates his adherence to truth and admits that his belief that one could escape was a cheat. He had allowed himself to be seduced and he now recognised the seductress as a *deceiving elf*. He ends by saying farewell to the nightingale, and with it the idea of escape, by deciding to stay in the real world and in doing so he describes the real ordinary landscape over which the bird flies.

> Adieu! adieu! thy plaintive anthem fades
> Past the near meadows, over the still stream,
> Up the hill-side; and now 'tis buried deep
> In the next valley-glades:

The nightingale has not simply flown but "is buried deep" just as Keats reminds us that we too will fade away and be buried. Perhaps he also decides, for the moment, to bury and mourn his omnipotence through which he was deceptively enjoying the illusion of immortality.

The ode ends with the question:

> Was it a vision, or a waking dream?
> Fled is that music:—Do I wake or sleep?

What matters here is that the music has fled. Keats is in silence now and he is for a time unsure what he is feeling. Is he conscious of the pain of loss or he is drugged as in the first stanza? There is even the possibility that he cannot hear the music because he is already dead with "ears in vain". We feel buoyed up by the beauty of the verse, perhaps aware that the poetry acts something like an opiate or deceiving elf to make the idea of death more bearable, and yet we are also stronger and more able to face the reality of our mortality.

Clinical example

Of course psychoanalysts are not poets; not only is our talent, training, and outlook different, but our task involves the everyday understanding of our patients rather than the discovery of universal poetic truths. Our situation is very different especially since, unlike the nightingale, the patient is a conscious, thinking human being who can answer and comment on any hypothesis that is made about him. His conflicts vary but tackling them brings us up against the deeper and more general conflict between facing and evading reality that Keats was exploring. Ultimately this forces us to confront the conflict between life and death and brings us up against our own mortality.[5]

Clinical material, Mr A

I am now going to take a look at some further material from Mr A, the patient discussed in Chapter 4, to see if I can differentiate the dual tasks that I have outlined. The patient began a Monday session two weeks before a summer break, saying,

> I am very aware that there are only two weeks left. I was going to say, until the break, but that assumes I am coming back, and I still might decide to stop. At the weekend I made contact with friends, I went to see my god-father and I spent some time with my parents. I felt a bit more normal.
>
> I also realised some things about myself. Something I can only call snob-bism, especially with Norman (his superior in his office). I am comfortable with people of my own class and not with certain others. I also have to come to terms with my attitude to black people. I noticed that a high pro-portion of people who drive aggressively are black and when I give way to a black driver they don't acknowledge me while I always wave a thank you when someone gives way to me. I am trying hard to say this in a way that will prevent you from jumping onto me and saying that I am racist.

I interpreted that the good weekend raised the possibility that he was improving but he thought I might be pleased at this and he did not want me to forget that he had reservations and might still end his analysis. I tried to empathise with his sense of improvement and added that feeling better may have made him realise that there were things about himself, like racism, that he did not like. If I jumped on him it would mean that I failed to remember his opposition to racism and snobbism.

To this he was impatient and irritable, saying, "I simply want you to look at the facts. It seemed to take us a long time to get anywhere. Why are you holding back? Why don't you address the substance of what I am saying?"

Further attempts to avoid provoking him were likewise met with irritation and he complained, "You are being too careful and not straightforward". I responded by a shift in hypothesis but one that I thought remained empathic, suggesting that he now wanted me to engage more directly in a confrontation in which one of us would have to back down. Perhaps he raised the question of road rage because he was aware of his fury with me, especially if I claimed he had improved.

He became more angry and strongly disagreed.

> I can't see where you get these ideas. It was not racism and had nothing to do with colour or class. The reason I became hostile was because Norman takes messages and does not acknowledge them. I can't stand the way my views are ignored.

I thought I had again missed something. Perhaps I had taken his message about the road rage but had failed to acknowledge that we were in the midst of a confrontation. Maybe one that could not be avoided but had to be experienced and lived through. I said that he saw me as someone who wanted my own way and that I expect him to submit. One of us had to climb down and then the other might be able to wave acknowledgement.

Discussion

Two main themes seemed to me to be discernible in the patient's material, one to do with a sense of improvement and development and the other connected with an angry confrontation involving rivalry, disappointment and accusations of unfairness. When I heard about his good weekend, I thought he was bringing a positive view of the analysis. I could empathise with the improvement and even assumed that feeling stronger he was able to reassess his attitudes especially towards Norman but also to black drivers, both of which had a resonance to his rivalry with me. He was always objecting to the way I handled issues around the setting including my coming break. Even when he mentioned that he might still terminate his analysis I was able to sustain what I felt was an empathic identification and understand that he did not want me to become complacent and satisfied with my work. I thought he was expressing some insight into his habitual preoccupation with status and hierarchy and I could sympathise with this view and could see his indignation as a healthy rebellion against authority.

It was not until he responded with impatience, and repeated his demand that I be more straightforward and address the substance of what he was saying that I began to suspect that my identification with an appreciative thoughtful patient suited me and that he might have moved into a different mood which, at that point, I was reluctant to accept. Gradually I developed the idea that his improvement might have led not to a concordance of view between us but to a strengthening of his willingness to rebel and fight for his independence. Only then was I able to withdraw my identification with the patient and sympathise with Norman and the black drivers. I could then see that we may have been in the midst of a confrontation that I had been trying to deny and to avoid. At last I realised that the road-rage situation, which had been latent from the beginning, was now uppermost. He could reasonably feel misunderstood if I spoke to the more cooperative patient I preferred to have, and ignored the angry resentful one who wanted to be heard. Eventually I became at least transiently able to move out of the empathic identification into a more real confrontation.

Another session

Two days later he told me a dream.

> I was at a modern art gallery standing in front of an exhibit of a tree root about 2 foot square with small rootlets sticking out looking untidy. I thought it needed pruning and I took out some secateurs and cut off a piece of root, which I put in my pocket. I was embarrassed and I sidled out of the museum hoping I would not be seen. Once out of the building I felt a relief thinking, they can't do anything to me now. I came across some secateurs in my flat yesterday. I always dead-head the flowers on my patio; my father says it is what they need.

I interpreted that he knew that he liked to improve on my work by tidying it up and that he felt free to clip the root even though it was in a museum. Maybe this would provoke me to criticise him and claim that the exhibit was mine and that he was attacking me by clipping away at the root. I added that his embarrassment as he put the rootlet in his pocket suggested that he knew there was something wrong going on.

He said,

> It reminded me of the email I got from the accountants saying, "where is the money?" I thought they have caught up with me at last. What is the worst they can do? I haven't stolen the money; it is all accounted for.

He had obtained a grant for a project with which he was due to reimburse the company but to get the money he had to write a report that he kept putting off.

"The report will blight my summer. I am tempted to pay the money out of my own pocket to avoid having to write it".

I suggested that I had misread his mood when I saw the snipping as an attack on my work. Going to the art gallery itself was quite an admission of his interest in our work, and even though he became embarrassed when he pocketed the rootlet he felt that, as with the accounts, he had done nothing wrong.

He agreed with this interpretation and went back to the dispute with Norman. "He is trying to cut me out of decision-making. I demanded to know if the office was hierarchical or collaborative. Norman sent a memo as if it came jointly from both of us. I told him, 'No!, this is not collaboration, it is you exercising your authority'".

I interpreted that he used his analysis to develop ideas of his own and that he saw me in rivalry holding to my own views and not listening to his. It was infuriating if I spoke as if we worked together and had similar views while he thought I was exercising authority and denying the hierarchy between us.

He said, "It is like people who spoil GM crops. They are accused of vandalism but it is a protest. It is outrageous to call it vandalism. When I failed my motorbike test in Germany I was furious because they made me slowly zigzag between cones with a pillion rider behind. It was so unfair because I have been riding a bike for years, and it was never a skill I would need. It is these bloody Germans! They think they own the roads!" After a short pause he said, "Of course you could say that the Germans do own their own roads".

I interpreted that he did not want to vandalise my work but he did want to make a protest. He could see that I claimed it was my consulting room and that I could dictate a structure where I determined issues like the holiday dates. Sometimes he accepted this but now he wanted to protest. Perhaps he saw me as making a display of my work as if it was art to be admired. To this he wanted to protest and even to claim that the achievements of the analysis were his to use as he thought fit.

Later I also interpreted that he found writing the report difficult because it made him feel that I was putting pressure on him to express his gratitude and to acknowledge that I had helped him. He did not want to fuel my narcissism through admitting that he admired my work. Only after he had been able to express his rage at "These bloody analysts, who think they own their consulting rooms", was he able to step back and concede that perhaps each of us had a point. Only after the confrontation could we each step down and wave an acknowledgement to each other.

Discussion

It seems to me that initially, in this second session, I perseverated with the theme of a confrontation assuming that he was attacking my work, claiming it was his property and even that he was stealing bits of it. Eventually I was able to move more flexibly in and out of the confrontations and in the process I thought we were each able to concede that the other could be partly right. This led to a kind of mutual climb down where we could wave acknowledgement, but only transiently. I was easily provoked to demand acknowledgement of my value and when I did this he thought I was exerting my superior status while all the time denying that there was a hierarchical difference between us. He did not like having me as a pillion rider sitting behind him because he felt observed and required to attend to me. He was furious that I saw this as an aspect of the setting but he could also smile ironically at his initial fury when he realised that Germans are entitled to own "their own roads". At these moments I think he could allow me to be a person in my own right and feel more entitled to be a separate person himself.

Flexible projective identification and irony

Irony is a view of life that recognises that experience is open to multiple interpretations, and making an ironic statement implies that we also believe its opposite (Fowler, 1926; Abrams, 1956; Muecke, 1970). I will discuss irony in more detail in Chapter 10 but here just point out that Keats was able to move in and out of identifications so effectively because he could claim one thing and at the same time imply another. A belief in immortality was held alongside the inevitability of death for example. This allowed him to move between imagination and reality without losing himself completely in one belief or the other. He seems to me to exemplify a capacity to be in touch with both reality and illusion, and this gives the verse a nuance of irony.

My patient initially had little potential for irony and could only accuse others of racism and unfairness. Later he was able to recognise his own arrogance and could smile as he admitted that perhaps the Germans did own their own roads. I thought that the rage had relented and that a capacity for irony had returned.

Both of us were prone to construct idealised phantasies of a peaceful cooperation between us, something like a Garden of Eden illusion in which the lion lies down with the lamb. Then when reality impinged we had to relinquish the idealisation and face the painful idea that the illusion was unreal. The illusion of closeness and harmony based on identification and empathy had then to be given up. I had to let the patient go, to tolerate his independence and to accept the loneliness, helplessness and depression associated with reality. Many of my ambitions had then to be buried deep in the next valley's glades.

Flexible projective identification and the primal scene

The need to be able to engage in a flexible projective identification arises early in life as the infant confronts the primal scene. The "window suddenly goes up"[6] (Sodre, 2017), or the curtain rises, to reveal the parents in a relationship with each other, presenting the infant with one of the earliest challenges to his omnipotence. Such experiences can be shocking and even traumatic and the child's ability to cope with them determines the form and outcome of the Oedipus Complex with its profound impact on the personality.

Normally what happens is that the infant recreates a version of the Garden of Eden Illusion believing that through the omnipotent possession of his mother every need will be met and that his bliss will go on forever. If he and his mother are unable to emerge from this early *folie à deux* a propensity for narcissistic illusions may make it more difficult to withdrawal from identifications in the future.

However the infant, and indeed all of us if we want a rich life, must also be willing to engage in flights of the imagination and enjoy omnipotent identifications to participate in heroic adventures (Campbell, 1949; Steiner, 2015): without them we are destined to live a restricted life in an evidence-based world.

Like Keats we have to recognise our need for illusion but ultimately to face the inevitability of loss, and to face the decisive test of our humanity, namely our acceptance of our mortality. Every time we enter the patient's mind through an act of sympathetic imagination we enjoy an illusion of closeness based on omnipotence, and every time we emerge to observe what we have been doing we have to face and mourn the loss of the illusion we have been enjoying. This is what Keats was able to do with such impressive success.

Notes

1 Another example of a similar process is provided by the biographer Richard Holmes who describes how he first identifies with his subject and only later and with reluctance and sadness, does he face the loss of the empathic understanding as he looks at his subject as an observer from the outside, (Holmes, 1995).

2 Nagel (1974), discusses the question of "What Is It Like to Be a Bat?" asking first what we might feel if we had webbing on our arms, which enabled us to fly catching insects in our mouth, with very poor vision, and perceiving the surrounding world by a system of reflected high-frequency sound signals, as well as hanging upside down by one's feet in an attic. He then points out that even as we try to imagine this we have to realise that it fails to tell us what it is like for a bat to be a bat, and the same limitations exist even when it is another human being we are observing.

3 Keats wrote his six odes between April and September 1819. He was 23.

4 The poetry creates resonances across 200 years of time, and is enhanced when we learn from Helen Vendler (1985), that the scene is not simply drawn from nature but based on Oberon's instructions to Puck in his search for a magic potion.

> I know a bank where the wild thyme blows,
> Where oxlips and the nodding violet grows,
> Quite over-canopied with luscious woodbine,
> With sweet musk-roses and with eglantine: ...
> (Midsummer Night's Dream, Act 2, Scene 1)

5 Segal (1952) in her discussion of aesthetic pleasure uses the term *nach-erleben*, borrowed from the philosopher Dilthey, (Hodges, 1944), which involves an unconscious reliving of the creator's state of mind. Segal suggests that this is achieved by an identification with the author and his internal world. Two factors are essential to the appreciation of a work, first the unshrinking expression of the full horror of the depressive phantasy and second the achieving of an impression of wholeness and harmony. Her discussion is very relevant to the present analysis of Keats work on the ode.

6 Sodre (2017), has pointed out that the Wolf Man begins his dream by stating, "Suddenly the window opened of its own accord, and I was terrified to see that some white wolves were sitting on the big walnut tree in front of the window".

8 The impact of trauma on the ability to face disillusion[1]

Facing the truth about ourselves is always traumatic and the relinquishment of an idealised Garden of Eden Illusion can plunge us into an unbearable situation even when it is revealed to involve nothing more terrible than facing the ordinary pains of reality. What then is the situation if the trauma of disillusion is more than just facing reality? There are cases when the real world can have an impact above and beyond the disillusion itself.

Of course the range of events that constitutes actual trauma is difficult to define but in cases of gross deprivation, violent attacks, and abuse, it seems obvious that an impingement beyond that of disillusion is taking place. Sophocles' *Oedipus the King* which has been discussed from the point of view of disillusion is also an example of trauma because of the dreadful mutilation of the infant Oedipus who had his feet pierced and was left to die. This aspect is rarely commented on by critics and is overlooked by both the participants in the drama and the observers of the tragedy.

The analyst has to be sensitive to the fact that the patient may experience the impact of ordinary reality as cruel but he must also recognise that some-times cruel events are imposed on the patient from the people around him that inflict a suffering that is beyond the normal expectation of reality. This means that an important aspect of reality involves the recognition that the world is not naturally good. Bad things happen and bad people inflict trau-mas that cannot be understood to result simply from disillusion.

The trauma inflicted on Oedipus

In the third day of his life Oedipus suffered a violent assault: his ankles were pierced and he was given to a shepherd with instructions to expose him to his death on Mt Cithaeron. Everyone in Thebes assumed he had per-ished but as it happened the shepherd took pity on the child and handed him over to a fellow shepherd from Corinth. This act of mercy eventually led not just to his life being saved but to his adoption as their son by the childless King Polybus and his Queen Merope of Corinth.

We must surely assume that the violent murderous assault inflicted a severe trauma on the defenceless three-day-old infant and one can only imagine the screams, the bleeding, and deformity of the ankles and the sense of disaster and tragedy that would have horrified any observer. Even though the imagination can provide a vivid scenario it is remarkable that the trauma has not featured prominently in discussion of the Oedipus Myth. Perhaps, as Davies (2012) has pointed out, this part of the Oedipus story is easy to overlook because we prefer to share the illusion rather than face the disturbing reality. Of course we do not know how a three-day-old baby experiences an assault of this kind but we no longer believe, as we used to do, that babies feel nothing and remember nothing. I think that we are obliged to assume that such trauma would have left a significant scar, both physical and psychological. As we read about the drama of Oedipus, most convincingly portrayed in Sophocles' play, but also in the wider myths that surround his life, we can use his story as a stimulus to ideas and hypotheses that may help us to understand our patients. In the present paper I hope that it can help us to explore the impact of trauma that has not been recognised or acknowledged.

An interesting feature in his story is the fact that the rescue by the shepherds not only saved Oedipus' life, but also transformed it into one of royal comfort. Indeed, like Adam and Eve he could enjoy his good fortune provided he did not ask too many questions in particular about anything that might lead him to discover his origins. He was adopted into the royal family of Corinth and it seems that his stepparents provided him with a loving home but took care to withhold knowledge of his background. Curiosity about the reason that his feet were scarred or why he had been given the name Oedipus, which means swollen foot, was suppressed.

At several points in his life Oedipus might have enquired about his origins but he either failed to do so or was successfully put off so that the disturbed and traumatic incidents of his infancy remained undiscovered and replaced by a view of loving parents to whom he remained devoted. The reader of the myth, however, knows something of the horrors of the circumstances of his conception and birth just as did the Greek audience of Sophocles' drama. These antedate Sophocles' play and amply document the tension between Laius and Jocasta, chiefly concerning their failure to have a child but probably also influenced by stories of Laius' homosexuality (Devereux, 1953; Graves, 1955; Stewart, 1961; Edmunds and Ingber, 1977; Davies, 2012; Zepf, Ulrich, and Seel, 2016). Laius consulted the Delphic Oracle over these difficulties and was given the dire prophecy that he was destined to be murdered by his son. To avoid this fate he turned away from Jocasta only to find that she tricked him into conceiving a child by getting him drunk. We can imagine the tense relations between them that followed this seduction and the ensuing pregnancy and moreover in the course of Sophocles play we learn that when the baby was born Jocasta was complicit in organising his death. It was she who handed him over to the shepherd after his feet had been pierced and it is left unclear whether she concurred with the need to eliminate the threat to the King or if she secretly arranged for him to survive or at least hoped he might do so.

Oedipus knew nothing of this history even though, at several points in the story he did have doubts that disturbed him. One day, taunted by a Corinthian youth that he did not in the least resemble his supposed parents, Oedipus travelled to Delphi to ask the oracle about his origins. Instead of the reassurance he expected to hear the oracle greeted him with the warning that he was cursed and destined to kill his father and marry his mother. Even though the purpose of his visit was to discover the truth about his parentage Oedipus ignored the fact that he failed to do so and remained convinced that Polybus and Merope were his parents and that he must flee Corinth to save them from murder and incest.

What happened next is that approaching Thebes at the famous junction where three roads meet, a carriage blocked his path and Oedipus was roughly ordered to step aside and make way for his betters. Oedipus was riled and retorted that he knew no betters except for the Gods and his own parents. The chariot drove on and one of the wheels bruised Oedipus's foot. In a rage he killed the charioteer, flung King Laius onto the road entangled in the reins, and whipping up the team, he made them drag him to his death. The violence of the response over an issue of status, the irony of the claim that he knew no betters except the Gods and his parents, and the bruising of his foot allows the observer to make connections with his original trauma in the hands of the same man. But Oedipus makes no such connection and even though he was warned just a few days earlier that he was destined to kill his father he murders a man of his father's age without compunction or subsequent anxiety.

Next, following his triumphant encounter with the Sphinx, he entered his fateful marriage to Jocasta where again no questions were raised that might link the murder of the King with the man he had just killed, and no connection was made by Jocasta between these scars on his feet and the trauma she was party to, or at least knew had been inflicted on her son: the very son who had been such a danger that he had to be got rid of. This failure to connect is evident right up to the climax of Sophocles' play when the truth finally emerged to reveal not only the cycle of trauma, revenge, and further trauma, but the defensive cover-up that had prevented questions from being asked. I have previously suggested that a collusion existed between Oedipus and the other participants of the tragedy to turn a blind eye to the facts of who Oedipus was, whom he had killed and whom he had married (Steiner, 1985). In this chapter I want to focus on the trauma experienced by Oedipus as a baby and the cover-up in which the infirmity of his ankles was ignored and its significance for his origins overlooked.

A phantasy of an ideal family as a defence against trauma

We can imagine a scenario in which the Royal Court of Corinth provided Oedipus with a haven in the form of a place of safety where the traumatised and inured infant could recover and grow up in a family where he was wanted and loved. My hypothesis is that he idealised his adoptive family and used this idealisation to overlook awkward questions about his origins and specifically to wipe out awareness and curiosity about the original trauma and its impact.

What we witness as the myth unfolds, brilliantly revealed in the course of Sophocles' play, is the striking way knowledge is hinted at, even spoken about by some of the participants, but is not taken up and not investigated. The result is the creation of a situation often used as an example of dramatic irony, in which the audience knows the facts that the protagonists are denying. This irony adds to the tension of the play and to the meaning of the denouement. Oedipus presents us with a picture of a normal, even ideal, family of his childhood in Corinth but this idealisation continues to be applied to his current family in Thebes despite the growing evidence that accumulates as the play proceeds. All the participants conspire to keep knowledge at bay and to avoid freeing up curiosity and pursuing the inquiry that would have shattered the idealised illusion. If we pay attention to the issue of infantile trauma we see that the scars, infirmities, and swellings of the feet, the doubts about parentage, and the original prophecy that led Laius to attempt to kill his son, have been disavowed, even though they are there in the background and certainly known to the audience. The significance of the trauma is buried and replaced by a scenario that is initially meant to reassure and later is submerged beneath the horror of Jocasta's death and Oedipus' guilt and self-blinding.

The Garden of Eden Illusion

In Chapter 1, I described how phantasies of an idealised time in which the infant has every wish gratified and is protected from frustration, disappointment and other unpleasant experiences seem to be universal. They are deeply embedded in our psyche in the form of the Garden of Eden and similar myths and are closely related to Freud's idea of a primary narcissism in which infantile omnipotence creates an illusion of "His Majesty the Baby". Freud suggests that the family typically colludes and even encourages the phantasy of omnipotence because of their own reluctance to face reality (Freud, 1914, p. 91).

Even though the idealisation is based on omnipotence and distorts the child's view of the real world Klein thought it was vital as a temporary measure to help to establish secure, loving, internal objects in relation to which the child can mature to the point where he can cope more readily with the hardships of reality. Winnicott (1953) also emphasised the importance of allowing the infant to have a period of omnipotent illusion even to the point when he believes that the breast is under his omnipotent control. It is not unusual for mothers to foster the illusion of a perfect couple and the wider family may tolerate the mutual idealisation even when it appears as a *folie à deux* for a considerable time (Steiner, 1997).

Disillusionment

Occasionally the patient believes he has achieved the bliss of these idyllic states and speaks of wonderful parents, the best possible marriage, or a perfect analysis, but mostly the Garden of Eden phantasy appears as a model against which actual experiences are judged and found wanting. The ideal phantasy is then viewed as one that might have been possessed if it were not for an unfair, premature, and sometimes cruel and brutal expulsion (Akhtar, 1996).[2] Such expulsions are invariable traumatic and particularly when sudden, unexpected and un-cushioned by sympathetic understanding, can be felt as a catastrophic betrayal. The patient may then strive to recreate the perfection and expect his analysis to undo the wrongful expulsion and to recreate the idealisation. This position can become entrenched, often to the analyst's despair, when giving up the retreat is experienced—or claimed to be—the horrible analyst trying to cruelly traumatise the patient into facing an unbearable reality. Here we need to recognise that both the intolerable guilt and also the plain unbearability of the abuse may lead to the entrenchment.

In normal circumstances, however, the infant does gradually overcome the trauma and relinquishes omnipotence in order to adapt to the new reality in which, despite the loss of the ideal, the facts of life are to a greater or lesser degree accepted. The difference between the normal and the pathological is illustrated in Milton's *Paradise Lost* (Steiner, 2013) where we can compare the fate of Adam and Eve on the one hand with that of Lucifer on the other. Both have been expelled from ideal situations but Adam and Eve painfully accept their expulsion from Eden, while Lucifer remains defiant in perpetual opposition to God. Segal (2007) pointed out that the terrible punishment inflicted on Adam and Eve turned out to be nothing more than to live in the real world, without the delusional comforts of Paradise. They were forced to suffer the pain of childbirth and obliged to work for their daily bread, and most of all to accept the reality of their eventual death. Despite their pain, guilt, and shame they accepted their fate and in the moving final stanza of his poem Milton describes them leaving Eden in sorrow but far from destroyed. By contrast Lucifer's expulsion from Heaven was too great a humiliation for him to accept and he remained in resentful opposition to God as he continued to harbour resentment and plan revenge.

To achieve an acceptance of reality is never easy and the infant requires the support of a mother who has both been able to tolerate the illusion and also gradually, "to disillusion the infant" (Winnicott, 1953, p. 95). In the same way the patient in analysis needs to have an analyst who can sympathetically support both the need for illusion and the need to relinquish it.

Real and damaging physical and mental trauma

Sometimes the trauma is so physically and mentally damaging that it is very difficult to come to terms with. The trauma may then present a view of the world in which cruelty and persecution actually exist and in which bad objects that previously existed in unconscious phantasy become real. It forces on us the recognition that the world contains predators, that violence may be unavoidable, and that the protective environment, which we were led to trust, can let us down. Severe trauma can arise from abuse, from the violence of wars and disasters, and also from bereavement and neglect when good objects have become unavailable. A particularly disturbing type of disillusion occurs when an infant has experienced a loving environment which is then suddenly lost if the mother remains present, but psychologically unresponsive and emotionally dead (Murray and Trevarthen, 1985; Green, 1986).

When external trauma is severe it breaks through the protective shield created by normal splitting, and a sense of betrayal arises when the good object is felt to have let the infant down and is discovered to be the very murderous persecutor that the splitting was meant to keep at bay. In these cases narcissistic defences based on omnipotent phantasies are deployed in attempts to recreate the idealisation and return to the state before disillusion occurred.

Sometimes, however, the impact of reality itself can be experienced as a disaster and may take the form of the child's reaction to a new baby in the family or even the recognition of the parent's relationship with each other. Even such ordinary events may be traumatic and to varying degrees they may come to represent not the ordinary reality of life but cruel, unjust, and damaging intrusions. In many cases phantasies of powerful narcissistic possession of the good object have been invoked and the omnipotence deployed to sustain the idealisation makes subsequent facing of reality and relinquishment of the illusion more difficult.

Sometimes the individual seems to be suspended at a choice point where a move in one direction enables a shift towards the depressive position in which the loss of the Garden of Eden is accepted and mourned. Moves in this direction are only possible if guilt is bearable and if guilt is not bearable a paranoid solution is likely to develop. Trauma inflicted by others shatters illusions abruptly and inexplicably and when it arises without any collusion from the victim it may make guilt more difficult to recognise and bear. It seems a paradox then that guilt is often described by the victims of trauma when it seems obvious that the guilt should belong to the perpetrator. Often guilt is linked to infantile phantasies of omnipotent power that long preceded the trauma and exploring these in someone who is the victim of trauma may be thought of as inappropriate and even unethical. Sometimes the victim tries to have his guilt understood and finds that everyone insists that all the guilt must be borne by the perpetrators so that moves towards the depressive position are delayed or avoided.

Universal general phantasies and specific abusing traumas

A degree of trauma as a result of disillusion is universal and is inflicted by all parents because the child, if he is to develop, must of necessity be expelled from the idealised Garden of Eden phantasy. Every father is then felt to abuse his children when he interferes with the idealised couple comprising the mother and the baby. However, even these ordinary everyday traumas can have damaging effects because of the unconscious phantasies they correspond to and severe disability may result from what seems to be minor trauma if resentment prevents the relinquishment of the Garden of Eden Illusion.

Such inevitable traumas however differ from the more exceptional traumas when violence and abuse is inflicted on a helpless victim. In the case of severe trauma we are not simply dealing with the inevitable impact of reality but rather with additional specific injuries that vary in severity as well as the context in which they are experienced. I think we must assume that if severe physical and mental abuse takes place we have an additional ingredient that leaves behind sequelae of a serious kind.

We do not know enough about these sequelae but one consequence seems to be that the idealised states that were mounted to protect the child from a premature invasion of ordinary reality now have to deal with the vastly more damaging and specific intrusion of external damage. It is understandable that in these cases more powerful and omnipotent defences are mounted which are less easy to relinquish. When reality is too extreme it may be unbearable both in the early stages when the organism is not yet equipped to cope with it and also later when too great a reliance on an idealised pathological organisation has developed.

When the trauma is actual, the truth that the patient has ultimately to face includes the realisation that cruel, damaging objects do exist and that the idealisation that has helped him to deny reality cannot be sustained. In the case of Oedipus the truth that eventually had to emerge included the fact that the illusion of his perfect family was a lie, and that his actual mother and father had cruelly abandoned him.

Oedipus as injured and vengeful

In the idealised image of Oedipus in the painting by Ingres[3] we can see that there is no sign of injury, as if the artist like everyone else turned a blind eye to the damaged feet. We do see a foot in the left-hand corner that probably represents one of the victims of the Sphinx, but might also be an unconscious reminder that feet should not be ignored.

If we give free rein to phantasy we can imagine the more paranoid situation that arises if the loss of the idealised illusion is so shattering that guilt cannot be faced by any of the parties, whether victim or perpetrator. In this version the effects of the trauma had not gone underground but remained conscious and created a more malign image of Oedipus, for example as a figure with a limp, physically and emotionally crippled by the piercing, and bearing a grudge against those who inflicted the injury on him. Perhaps like Shakespeare's Richard III he then sees himself as injured and deformed:

not shaped for sportive tricks,
Nor made to court an amorous looking-glass;[4]

Instead of suppressing the trauma and his vengeful reaction to it Oedipus might then have been able to give conscious vent to his wish for violent revenge.

And therefore, since I cannot prove a lover,
To entertain these fair well-spoken days,
I am determined to prove a villain
And hate the idle pleasures of these days.
    (Shakespeare, 1592–1594, *Richard III*,
                Act 1 Scene 1)

Resentful about having been brought deformed into the world Oedipus in this thought experiment was full of hatred of his parents and of authority figures in general. His fury towards his adoptive parents for withholding the facts of his injury was augmented when the oracle also failed to provide him with the truth giving him only a threatening message that filled him with fear. Then when he meets Laius at the crossroads we can better understand the violence of his over-reaction to being asked to step aside by a figure of authority. The clash led to a defeat of the father and victory for the son and might have enabled guilt for this act to have brought the destructive process to a halt. However in the circumstances, this guilt could not be accepted by Oedipus particularly in the absence of a supportive figure who might help him bear the terrible truth. Instead Jocasta put up no obstacles to the marriage and persuaded him to ignore the prophecy which she repeatedly argued was not to be trusted. This meant that like Richard III, he was able to marry the woman whose husband he had just killed.

One could make out a case for the idea that Oedipus was a man disappointed in his fate and responding with fury and vengeance when the truth was denied him. Finally we can imagine that he came to believe that no one could love him if they knew his history, namely who he was, what had been done to him, and what he had done. This meant that he had no sense of goodness within and chose to triumph over those who had traumatised him and to seek success through power rather than love.

This type of reconstruction may seem fanciful but I believe it is of value because it seems so precisely to represent the type of unconscious phantasy world that severely traumatised patients have to negotiate. It helps us to understand the role of guilt when we recognise the undercurrent of injury, resentment and violent revenge that trauma leaves behind in the unconscious mind.

The discovery and abandonment of the seduction theory

Freud's early theories gave trauma a central role as a cause of hysteria. At that time he used a rather mechanical model in which the traumatic event was to be identified and purged from an overburdened psyche in the course of treatment. Early descriptions used the image of over-stimulation leading to a piercing of a protective shield so that anxiety and excitement could not be mastered and bound but remained unmodified and continued to create a damaging effect existing like a foreign body in the psyche.

A major shift in the conception of trauma took place when Freud abandoned the seduction theory. In his famous letter to Fliess he seems to have realised the importance of the moment because he said:

> I will confide in you at once the great secret that has been slowly dawning on me in the last few months. I no longer believe in my neurotica.
>   Certainly I shall not tell it in Dan or speak of it in Askelon, in the land of the Philistines.
>
> (Freud, 1897)[5]

To begin with Freud felt bereft and confused, and perhaps even traumatised, confessing that, "Now I have no idea of where I stand" (Freud, 1897). His theory was dead and he did not want to give his enemies ammunition to attack him with. Having worked so hard to shift the prevailing view of the aetiology of mental disorders from its preoccupation with heredity and degeneration to a consideration of mental conflicts he now had to face the fact that his work had received a serious blow. However, as with some of his other setbacks, for example, the discovery of transference, the reversal enabled him to go forward to make new discoveries. He told Fliess that he thought his doubts about trauma might actually result in an advance towards further insight.

Freud continued to believe that trauma was significant in hysteria but he added the idea that the phantasy life of the child was also important. In 1906 he wrote:

> They [Hysterical symptoms] were no longer to be regarded as direct derivatives of the repressed memories of childhood experiences; but between the symptoms and the childish impressions there were inserted the *patient's fantasies.*
>
> (Freud, 1906, p. 274)

Some writers have considered that this shift implied that Freud no longer believed that trauma was significant and that he wished only to cover up the terrible facts of child abuse. Masson (1984) and others even argued that in repudiating the seduction theory, "truth was suppressed in favour of a socially palatable lie" (Makari, 1998, p. 897). While it should be evident that the introduction of the patient's phantasies between the repressed memories of trauma and the hysterical symptoms does not deny the importance of trauma, I think it is right to observe that the change led to a shift in the focus of analytic work from that of identifying the traumatic event to the more complex discovery of the phantasies that gave it meaning.

From our contemporary perspective we can now see that relinquishment of the seduction theory was the beginning of psychoanalysis as we understand it today. It led to the recognition of the existence of an internal world of unconscious phantasy including infantile sexuality, and the Oedipus complex, and far from reducing the importance of trauma it made it potentially more comprehensible in the context of an interaction between external trauma and internal pre-existing and reactive phantasies. No longer preoccupied with the search for traumatic memories the task for the analyst became that of trying to receive and understand both verbal and non-verbal communications from his patient and to recognise how trauma was experienced and responded to. With the discovery of the importance of transference the task could be more precisely defined as that of discovering the unconscious phantasy that determined the way the patient perceived his analyst and reacted to him. Verbal accounts of abuse and neglect of course remain important as evidence of trauma but our knowledge also depends on the patient's experience of the transference and the enactment of phantasies that allow us to explore the various factors that give meaning to trauma.

These considerations are relevant to the more general problem of giving appropriate weight both to external influences that impinge on the patient and to internal phantasies that influence the perceived meaning of external events. Both are clearly important but one or other can dominate in a particular instance. This means that the interaction between external objects and those in the internal world leads to a complex relationship between them that can only gradually be clarified through careful analysis of the transference.

The significance of unconscious guilt for psychic change

The role of guilt in traumatised patients is problematic both for the analyst and for the patient. If a patient has been abused, assaulted and traumatised it is natural for him to feel resentment, hatred, and a wish for justice and revenge, so that to feel guilt seems to be out of place. People tend to take up extreme positions towards guilt. If you believe that all the guilt should be felt by the perpetrator of trauma then exploring the guilt felt by the victim may seem to repeat the trauma originally inflicted on him. In other cases patients masochistically accept guilt for everything that has happened, denying the trauma and preferring to see their objects as good rather than abusive. Such extreme positions tend to focus on wrongdoing and try to identify who was responsible for it. They usually ignore the unconscious phantasies that surround the experience, including the context in which the abuse took place as well as the reactions to the abuse made by the victim. If these are considered it is possible to explore a more nuanced situation and to understand how guilt might arise in both parties.

I have also described how fear of embarrassment, shame, and humiliation can interfere with the emergence of guilt, and shame is certainly prominent when Garden of Eden Illusions are lost, as was the case in the expulsion of Adam and

Eve. Sometimes the ideal is concretely felt to be sustained by a phallic omnipotence and its loss is felt as a theft or castration. In fact Rosemary Davies (2012) has described shame in situations involving castration anxiety and suggests that for Oedipus it may have been part of his reaction to the original trauma. A preoccupation with shame may then make guilt difficult to examine and development may be blocked unless the patient can find the support to tackle, first the shame and then the guilt that lies beneath it (Steiner, 2015). It is important that the guilt is neither exaggerated nor minimised but is recognised as appropriate to the truth of what happened. If the guilt can be faced it is often a great relief to the patient and indeed often turns out to be less severe than his unconscious phantasies implied. Most important it can open the door to new developments in which persecution lessens as guilt gives rise to regret, remorse, and the wish to make reparation. However this can only happen if the patient can face a complex situation in which he accepts responsibility for what he has done without denying the guilt of others. This means that the truth has to be explored in detail as it is re-lived in the transference in order that guilt and blame can be properly apportioned. When the background details of both the victim and perpetrator are be examined their motives can be better understood and attenuating circumstances can come to moderate hatred.

Examining guilt presents severe technical difficulties and remains an issue that needs further research and exploration. While it does involve facing the truth and accepting the reality of what has happened it is not always clear what that truth is. Nor is it clear how the analyst should deal with his own guilt as he inevitably enacts at least some elements of the traumatic situation. As we saw in Chapter 2, it is also important to remember that when the truth is revealed it can be extremely cruel and reality itself can inflict a trauma that may be re-experienced in an unbearable form (Steiner, 2016).

It is therefore understandable that we find patients taking steps to accept their guilt but also having to evade it when it becomes unbearable. This was the situation in the case of Oedipus who is seen denying his guilt for most of Sophocles' play but eventually facing it with great courage and clarity at its climax when he could acknowledge that:

> I stand revealed at last:
> cursed in my birth, cursed in marriage,
> cursed in the lives I cut down with these hands!
> (Sophocles, 5th century BC, p. 238)

When the idealised phantasy that protected Oedipus from the facts collapsed the guilt was extreme and when he saw the hanged body of Jocasta it becomes unbearable. Having cut down her body he took her broaches and used them to put out his eyes in an act of horrifying self-mutilation in which he seemed to be identified with a punitive, cruel super-ego. It was particularly damaging because it destroyed his capacity to recover and face the task of atoning for his guilt and making reparation.

If we were to imagine exploring guilt with a patient like Oedipus, we would first have to protect him from any tendency to feel guilt for the original trauma. He did not order the piercing of his own feet and the fact that his existence threatened his father was no fault of the new-born baby.

Some guilt might emerge over the way he turned a blind eye or over his suppressed hatred that led to such a violent reaction to Laius when they met but the overwhelming contribution to guilt comes from the unconscious phantasies that are revealed as reality begins to be faced. If we accept that Oedipus, like anyone else, harboured unconscious phantasies of killing his father as an expression of his wish for a blissful union with his mother, then the actual murder of his father corresponded with the unconscious wish and it is guilt over this wish that is so difficult to accept. Even more traumatic perhaps was the phantasy only revealed with the collapse of the Garden of Eden Illusion, that he also hated his mother but that this hatred had been split off and disavowed through the idealisation.

However we must also remember that while trauma is to some degree inevitable and universal it is always to some degree damaging and not to be accepted as harmless. It is sometimes difficult for the analyst to retain a sympathetic understanding of the pain of disillusion and at the same time support the patient to accept that portion of guilt that is rightly his. The conflict generated may be particularly difficult for the analyst when the trauma has been re-lived in the transference and the analyst has to examine and take responsibility for his own errors and enactments.

A major consequence of reparative work is that good objects are restored to the patient's internal world and the super-ego becomes less fantastic and less persecutory. However alongside this, good objects are more realistically appraised so that bad elements are accepted as real rather than the result of paranoid projections. Paradoxically an element of reparation is to see bad objects as really bad and bad things to have really happened. The real world can then be seen as a mixed environment peopled by protective, caring, and nourishing figures but also containing violent predators, and that even our good objects contain elements of both. True reparation does not then recreate ideal objects but accepts real ones and strengthens the capacity to discriminate between them

However we must also recognise that some traumas inflict damage over and beyond the sense of disillusionment and loss of idealisation. The horrendous traumas of physical and sexual abuse leave specific scars behind that create additional damage that we often fail to understand. I have raised the possibility that if trauma is too severe it may make guilt impossible to accept and that this denies the subject of access to the benevolent cycle that leads from guilt to the capacity to mourn and to make reparation (Klein, 1957; Weiss, 2017).

Disillusion and *Nachträglichkeit*

These considerations raise the possibility that the interposition of a defensive Garden of Eden Illusion is one reason for the existence of *Nachträglichkeit* in which a delay exists between the timing of an original trauma and its manifest effect on the individual. Could it not be that, in some situations, the initial trauma has been so effectively covered up by the idealised illusion that it appears to have little effect until a subsequent event awakens the trauma and reveals the full impact of the disaster? This seems to have been the case with Oedipus who was initially able to ignore his injury and to evade all inquiry into its meaning. Later when the confrontation with Laius bruised his feet a second time he responded with uncontrolled violence and later still when the illusion finally broke down he had to face the catastrophe of his guilt, including that for Jocasta's death. When the disillusion finally came it exposed the cover-up and revived the original trauma giving it new meaning.

When the illusion is finally shattered the trauma appears *Nachträglich*, as a deferred action or *après coup*, because the impact can no longer be denied. Moreover in the new situation that arises, defensive illusions are no longer blinding him to the facts, so that now both the original trauma and the guilt associated with it can begin to be worked through. Always however with the proviso that the guilt is bearable, and without this a return to denial, idealisation and omnipotence are inevitable.

Notes

1 Based on: Steiner, J. (2018b) The Trauma and Disillusionment of Oedipus. *International Journal of Psychoanalysis*, 99, 555–568.
2 Akhtar (1996) has described "if only" and "someday" phantasies which are related to Garden of Eden Illusions. "If only" the shattering event had not occurred the illusion would still be alive, while "someday" implies that the wrong will be magically undone and the idealisation restored. Akhtar attributes these to a failure of disillusionment keeping a phantasy of an idealised state alive.
3 The idealised image of Oedipus (Ingres, 1805–1827), used to be shown on the cover of the International Journal, I suppose to represent the spirit of enquiry that solved the riddle of the sphinx. There are several different versions, one in the National Gallery in London and the best known in the Louvre.
4 For example in the image of Richard III played by Antony Sher (1984) who had obvious deformities and used crutches.
5 Here he was misquoting the reaction of King David to the death of Saul.

> The beauty of Israel is slain upon thy high places:
> how are the mighty fallen!
> Tell it not in Gath,
> publish it not in the streets of As'kelon;
> lest the daughters of the Philistines rejoice,
> lest the daughters of the uncircumcised triumph.

9   Learning from Don Quixote[1]

In his great novel *Don Quixote*, Cervantes describes the countless ways that his hero tries to impose his day-dreams onto the world around him. This is precisely what many of our patients do and the same is true of course for all of us since we are all patients and all have serious problems with reality. So although I am discussing a character from a novel my approach is clinical and I pick out ways I have found that we as psychoanalysts can learn from *Don Quixote*. Perhaps I will begin with a shocking feature of the book, also remarked on by others (Nabokov, 1984), and this is the degree of violence, cruelty, and especially humiliation that is heaped on the hapless knight. Each of the numerous adventures that Don Quixote embarks on ends in defeat and beginning with mockery and proceeding to physical pummelling and bruising, all those around him react to his madness with hostility and ridicule. Even Cervantes himself repeatedly mocks Don Quixote's madness, for example, when he describes him as a madman whose wits were gone.

> In short, his wits being quite gone, he hit upon the strangest notion that ever madman in this world hit upon, and that was that he fancied it was right and requisite, as well for the support of his own honour as for the service of his country, that he should make a knight-errant of himself, roaming the world over in full armour and on horseback ... righting every kind of wrong, ... to reap eternal renown and fame.
> (Cervantes, 1605a, Vol. 1, Chapter I, para. 4)[2]

Once he is labelled as mad Don Quixote is marginalised and both his friends and his enemies feel entitled to dismiss his personal dignity and to look down on him and mock him from a position of superiority. Initially we join in the laughter but then, as the irony hits us, we feel ashamed of our complicity in the cruelty. Complex feelings of admiration and eventually of love are allowed to emerge intermingled with anxiety and guilt.

The uncomfortable mixture of feelings helps us to become aware of the complexity of the reactions that illusion and madness may provoke in us. Usually we respond with a sympathetic understanding of our patients' suffering but sometimes, if psychotic elements in our own makeup have not been accepted, we can disown our own madness and look down on the disturbed patient from a position of superiority. When we find ourselves describing a person as disturbed, perverse, or immature we may not realise how humiliating it may feel to be labelled that way. Cervantes helps us to recognise that when this happens we are in Don Quixote's territory. He even links the humiliation of Don Quixote to the way unwanted members of society were treated by the inquisition and this cannot but remind the modern reader of the holocaust. Nabokov (1984) was so disturbed by the cruelty meted out to Don Quixote that he likened it to the humiliation and crucifixion of Christ. This comparison was also made earlier by Dostoevsky (1868), who saw Don Quixote as a religious figure.

> The main idea of the novel is to present a positively beautiful man. ... There is only one positively beautiful person in the world, Christ, and ... of all the beautiful individuals in Christian literature, one stands out as the most perfect, Don Quixote. But he is beautiful only because he is ridiculous. ... Wherever compassion toward ridiculed and ingenious beauty is presented, the reader's sympathy is aroused. The mystery of humour lies in this excitation of compassion.
>
> (Quoted by Loseff, 1998)

These thoughts are not entirely clear to the modern reader but I wonder if these writers saw beauty in the dignified way that Don Quixote suffered humiliation and in the compassion it evoked.

Burning of the books

Don Quixote's friends, the curate and barber together with his housekeeper and niece, decide to eliminate the malign influence of the tales of Chivalry by burning his books while he is asleep. In a parody of the inquisition they put each volume on trial, condemning most but saving a few that they personally enjoyed. Some books are spared by accident and some burned without being looked at. They also find a section of poetry and at first consider "pardoning" these until they are persuaded by the niece that nothing would be worse than to have her uncle succumbing to the "incurable and infectious malady" of poetry. Finally "the curate was tired and would not look into any more books, and so he decided that, 'contents uncertified,' all the rest should be burned" (Cervantes, 1605a, Vol. 2, Chapter VI, para. 39)

Later they seal and plaster over the door to his library to make it appear as if it had never existed. All evidence of the crime that had been committed was removed and responsibility for the incursion was denied in the manner of holocaust deniers.

I found these episodes to act as a telling reminder for the psychoanalyst to take account of the patient's right to his own views however eccentric, unusual or deluded they may seem. It warns us of an almost inevitable tendency to become self-appointed spokesmen for sanity and like the curate and barber to attempt to force reality onto a reluctant patient.

The ironic attitude

When we compare Don Quixote's chivalrous vision with the contemporary reality that is put forward as superior, we find the champions of reality to be conformist, unadventurous, and fearful of incurring disapproval. Cervantes knew what happens if you challenge authority. He was constantly in financial difficulty, he spent time in prison, he was wounded in the famous battle of Lepanto, and he spent years as a slave in North Africa. Moreover the forcible conversion and expulsion of Arabs and Jews and the tortures and executions carried out by the inquisition were a constant reminder of the cruelty of the current world controlled by authorities that were too powerful to be opposed by ordinary means. Through irony an apparently conformist comment can conceal a hidden opposition. We have seen the poet Cervantes describe poetry as an "incurable and infections malady" and later we hear Don Quixote's squire Sancho Panza assert his piety by declaring that he is a mortal enemy of the Jews.

> Since I believe, as I always do, firmly and truly in God, and all the holy Roman Catholic Church holds and believes, and that I am a mortal enemy of the Jews, the historians ought to have mercy on me and treat me well in their writings.
>
> (Cervantes, 1605a, Vol. 2, Chapter VIII, para. 12)

Irony enables the tolerance of contradictory views and offers a smile of insight when we see that neither view is completely true. When we apply this to the gap between the patient's view and that of the analyst an ironic stance can help the analyst to recognise that they may not be as different as at first seemed.

As we come to understand the origin and defensive purpose of Don Quixote's phantasy world it seems less foreign and less threatening. His madness remains unyielding but we come to see some virtue in it and we can admire his willingness to make a protest against a cruel reality which our propensity to conform prevents us from joining.

The Golden Age and the Garden of Eden Illusion

Don Quixote, like many who succumb to a Garden of Eden Illusion (Steiner, 2016, 2018a; Akhtar, 1996), regrets the passing of the Golden Age and sees it as his duty to undo the worst excesses of the evil that he sees all around him. In a long speech to some goatherds, abbreviated here, he describes the Golden Age in the following terms:

Happy the age, happy the time, to which the ancients gave the name of golden, ... because they that lived in it knew not the two words "mine" and "thine"!

In that blessed age all things were in common; to win the daily food no labour was required of any save to stretch forth his hand and gather it from the sturdy oaks....

Then all was peace, all friendship, all concord; as yet the dull share of the crooked plough had not dared to rend and pierce the tender bowels of our first mother that without compulsion yielded from every portion of her broad fertile bosom all that could satisfy, sustain, and delight the children that then possessed her.

Then was it that the innocent and fair young shepherdess roamed from vale to vale and hill to hill, with flowing locks, and no more garments than were needful modestly to cover what modesty seeks and ever sought to hide.

Maidens and modesty, as I have said, wandered at will alone and unattended, without fear of insult from lawlessness or libertine assault, and if they were undone it was of their own will and pleasure.

But now in this hateful age of ours not one is safe, not though some new labyrinth like that of Crete conceal and surround her; even there the pestilence of gallantry will make its way to them ... and, despite of all seclusion, lead them to ruin.

In defence of these, as time advanced and wickedness increased, the order of knights-errant was instituted, to defend maidens, to protect widows and to succour the orphans and the needy.

(Cervantes, 1605a, Vol. 1, Chapter XI, para. 6)

For Don Quixote the Golden Age is a phantasy of a pre-oedipal existence where the purity of the mother had not yet been violated and involves an illusion of an idealised infant–mother couple which requires protection from envious attacks. The fact that those who lived then did not know the difference between "thine and mine" suggests a lack of separateness between mother and child where everything the mother possessed was also his. The term "pestilence of gallantry" implies a sexual contamination and it seems clear that Don Quixote is attempting to keep sexual and aggressive wishes out of his mind by attributing them to others (Sodre, 2013). However the projections keep threatening to return to spoil the idealisation and in much of the novel he is engaged in endless battles against wrong-doers. There is something both noble and mad in his determination to protect the vulnerable and we are moved by his simplicity and constancy.

It is the paradox of the dignity of his madness that the novel explores in a myriad of ways, often brought out through the complex relationship that develops with Sancho Panza. The nobility of Don Quixote's ideals is in sharp contrast to those of Sancho whose desires are firmly tied to his appetites which keep him firmly rooted in reality. There is however an ironic twist because his reason gives way when he is offered the governorship of an island which he cannot resist and towards which he becomes even more gullible than his master.

The quest for admiration

The contrast between his pretentious phantasy world and the reality of Don Quixote's actual ineptness, weakness, and preposterous appearance becomes a source of endless laughter and ridicule. The fact that he is universally looked down on makes him determined to create a situation where he is admired and looked up to, even if he is obliged to articulate the admiration for himself. On his very first sortie, even before he has met a single adversary Don Quixote imagines how his praises will be sung.

> "Scarce had the rubicund Apollo spread o'er the face of the broad spacious earth the golden threads of his bright hair, scarce had the little birds of painted plumage attuned their notes to hail with dulcet and mellifluous harmony the coming of the rosy Dawn, that, ... the renowned knight Don Quixote of La Mancha, quitting the lazy down, mounted his celebrated steed Rocinante and began to traverse the ancient and famous Campo de Montiel"; which in fact he was actually traversing. "Happy the age, happy the time", he continued, "in which shall be made known my deeds of fame, worthy to be moulded in brass, carved in marble, limned in pictures, for a memorial for ever".
>
> (Cervantes, 1605a, Vol. 1, Chapter II, para. 2)

The over-blown language invites ridicule but also pity as it is clear that Don Quixote deals with feelings of vulnerability and inferiority in his phantasy of being admired. When he creates the absurd caricature of his glorious success it is not difficult to think of him as a child whose attempts at superiority only make him seem more childish and more ridiculous. When this happens in a normal family the mother's love can save the day if she can persuade the child that he does not need to be admired because he is loved. But Don Quixote has no one to do this, and instead, in every adventure, he ends up physically bruised and mentally humiliated. It is perhaps not so surprising that when he despairs of being loved he turns to admiration in its place.

The idealised object of his love

In imitation of the Knights of Chivalry, Don Quixote creates a character for himself of heroic proportions and he also creates an idealised image of a perfect lady, the peerless Dulcinea del Toboso, who serves as his ideal.

he came to the conclusion that nothing more was needed now but to look out for a lady to be in love with; for a knight-errant without love was like a tree without leaves or fruit, or a body without a soul.

(Cervantes, 1605a, Vol. 1, Chapter I, para. 8)

It turns out that Dulcinea is not a pure invention but a transformation of someone real, a peasant girl from a neighbouring village. Even though he is completely dedicated and loyal in his devotion to his ideal he is sufficiently in touch with reality to be aware of the fantastic nature of his beliefs. His awareness of the real world emerges when he lets slip that the peerless Dulcinea, described as a rich princess of beauty and stature is unable to read. He has written a letter that Sancho is to have copied and he explains why the handwriting is not important.

As to the love letter thou canst put by way of signature, "Yours till death, the Knight of the Rueful Countenance". And it will be no great matter if it is in some other person's hand, for as well as I recollect Dulcinea can neither read nor write, nor in the whole course of her life has she seen handwriting or letter of mine, for my love and hers have been always platonic, not going beyond a modest look, and even that so seldom that I can safely swear I have not seen her four times in all these twelve years I have been loving her ... and perhaps even of those four times she has not once perceived that I was looking at her: such is the retirement and seclusion in which her father Lorenzo Corchuelo and her mother Aldonza Nogales have brought her up.

(Cervantes, 1605a, Vol. 1, Chapter XXV, para. 41)

Sancho Panza is amazed and amused by this revelation.

"So, so!" said Sancho; "Lorenzo Corchuelo's daughter is the lady Dulcinea del Toboso, otherwise called Aldonza Lorenzo?"

"She it is", said Don Quixote, "and she it is that is worthy to be lady of the whole universe".

"I know her well", said Sancho, "and let me tell you she can fling a crowbar as well as the lustiest lad in all the town".

(Cervantes, 1605a, Vol. 1, Chapter XXV, para. 43)

Don Quixote admits that she is an imaginative creation but explains that this is also the case of all of the idealised figures of antiquity.

It is not to be supposed that all those poets who sang the praises of ladies under the fancy names they give them, had any such mistresses. Thinkest thou that the Amarillises, the Phillises, the Sylvias, the Dianas, the Galateas, the Filidas, and all the rest of them, that fill the books, the ballads, the barber's shops, the theatres are full of, were really and truly ladies of flesh and blood, and mistresses of those that glorify and have glorified them? Nothing of the kind; they only invent them for the most part to furnish a subject for their verses, and that they may pass for lovers, or for men valiant enough to be so; I persuade myself that all I say is as I say, neither more nor less, and I picture her in my imagination as I would have her to be, as well in beauty as in condition.

(Cervantes, 1605a, Vol. 1, Chapter XXV, para. 46)

So he admits that he sees what he wants to see, and that Dulcinea is a princess only in his imagination. However this in no way diminishes his belief in her existence and it enables him to pass for a lover and to seem valiant enough to do so.

The condescension and disdain of the ideal object

Don Quixote's phantasies are based on stories of Chivalry but also on unconscious phantasies of his early relationship with an idealised breast. He recreates an image of a needy infant waiting for his mother to return as he complains about Dulcinea's cruelty and neglect, driving him mad by leaving him in uncertainty of her love. He asks Sancho to describe the details of his suffering to Dulcinea to bear witness to her cruelty. As proof of his madness he bangs his head against the rocks and performs summersaults naked below the waist.

and pulling off his breeches in all haste he stripped himself to his skin and his shirt, and then, without more ado, he cut a couple of gambados in the air, and a couple of somersaults, heels over head, making such a display that, not to see it a second time, Sancho wheeled Rocinante round, and felt easy, and satisfied in his mind that he could swear he had left his master mad.

(Cervantes, 1605a, Vol. 1, Chapter XXV, para. 68)

One can't help being reminded of a toddler showing off his nakedness but Don Quixote is inordinately proud of this ridiculous portrayal of his madness.

[It is] an achievement wherewith I shall win eternal name and fame throughout the known world; and it shall be such that I shall thereby set the seal on all that can make a knight-errant perfect and famous.

(Cervantes, 1605a, Vol. 1, Chapter XXV, para. 12)

It is his courage and fortitude in the face of suffering that he believes will move the heart of Dulcinea to relent.

If thy beauty despises me, if thy worth is not for me, if thy scorn is my affliction, though I be sufficiently long-suffering, hardly shall I endure this anxiety, which, besides being oppressive, is protracted. My good squire Sancho will relate to thee in full, fair ingrate, dear enemy, the condition to which I am reduced on thy account: if it be thy pleasure to give me relief, I am thine; if not, do as may be pleasing to thee; for by ending my life I shall satisfy thy cruelty and my desire. Thine till death, The Knight of the Rueful Countenance.

> (Cervantes, 1605a, Vol. 1, Chapter XXV, para. 49)

We have a picture of an idealised good object but one that withholds love and compassion and has become his "fair ingrate" and "dear enemy". Don Quixote created a phantasy world built around an idealised object but one who is real enough to remind him of early frustrations, deprivations and betrayals. Love is then replaced by hurt, and a desire for revenge threatens to invade the idealisation and introduce hatred alongside the love. It is ironic to find ourselves sympathising with Don Quixote even though we have just been told that both the love and the suffering are figments of his imagination.

Here we see both the madness and the beauty of romantic love in which the unreality stems from the illusion that we have found the original ideal object of our infancy. For me the moment is especially poignant since it hints at the possibility of a transformation of romantic love with its illusion of perfection into a more realistic loving relationship. However, such a transformation which would involve ambivalence is clearly too much for Don Quixote to envisage. It would mean accepting both love and hate towards a good object and tolerating the idea that the destructiveness he was dedicated to combat also came from within himself. For Don Quixote this route towards sanity was not possible because his equilibrium depended on the continuing existence of the ideal object, and real suffering, real cruelty, real destructiveness were not just denied and projected but were clothed in unreality, idealisation, and eroticisation. In this way he finds an artful solution reminiscent of Freud's model of fetishism (Freud, 1927): he incorporates the ambivalence, cruelty, and melancholia into the phantasy, idealising it all as part of the romance (Sodre, 2012).

The helmet of Mambrino

Cervantes shows how the gap between phantasy and reality is managed when he describes the way Don Quixote uses his armour to create a shield or carapace to protect him from reality. However from the beginning the absence of a visor to his helmet means that there is a gap in his shell through which reality can enter. Without the visor he is exposed to both "seeing and being seen" (Steiner, 2011). If he is seen he is in danger of being unmasked as an ordinary mortal rather than a heroic knight and if he is able to see he can no longer avoid seeing reality for what it is. Ironically he prefers to look ridiculous in his attempts to sustain his illusions rather than to be exposed to the truth of his ordinariness.

This battle to protect himself from reality which we have seen he both recognised and then repudiated, is established at the very start of the novel. In the famous opening paragraph Cervantes describes his hero's everyday life as one of ordinariness and boredom.

> In a village of La Mancha, the name of which I have no desire to call to mind, there lived not long since one of those gentlemen that keep a lance in the lance-rack, an old buckler, a lean hack, and a greyhound for coursing.
>
> (Cervantes, 1605a, Vol. 1, Chapter I, para. 1)

He decides to leave this ordinary world of relative ease, boredom, and stagnation and to take on the identity of a knight-errant based on the tales of Chivalry that he has become obsessed with.

> The first thing he did was to clean up some armour that had belonged to his great-grandfather, and had been for ages lying forgotten in a corner eaten with rust and covered with mildew. He scoured and polished it as best he could, but he perceived one great defect in it, that it had no closed helmet, nothing but a simple morion. This deficiency, however, his ingenuity supplied, for he contrived a kind of half-helmet of pasteboard which, fitted on to the morion, looked like a whole one.
>
> (Cervantes, 1605a, Vol. 1, Chapter I, para. 5)

When he tests the visor with his sword he is disappointed to see it crumble but undaunted he makes a second visor reinforced with strips of iron and this time he wisely decides not to test it, declaring it to be extremely fine.

He is aware that his phantasy world cannot survive the impact of reality and decides not to put it to the test. We are reminded of Freud's (1924) suggestion that a delusion can serve as a patch to cover the rent that had opened up between the ego and the external world. Perhaps the visor to the helmet had a similar function.

Refusing to remove the helmet

The helmet becomes a special problem when Don Quixote arrives at an inn, which he misrepresents as a castle, and is helped to take off his armour by two women of easy virtue who he decides are gracious ladies. The helmet is tied on with green ribbon and he refuses to have it removed so that pieces of food have to be put in his mouth by the ladies while he holds the makeshift visor up with both hands. Moreover drinking is impossible until the landlord makes a straw out of a reed and pours wine into his mouth. Here in his stubbornness he is at his most babyish, as if in a high chair having to be hand-fed by the "ladies" and to drink through a straw. He needs the visor to protect him from reality but in doing so he reveals how infantile he feels.

This scene is a source of great hilarity to the company and is typical of the ridicule which the hero meets in each of his adventures. The narrator, and in many situations his friends too, join in the ridicule which Don Quixote mostly bears with great dignity and fortitude. For the reader however the cruelty and especially the humiliation meted out to the deluded knight begins to give the mockery a bitter taste.

Later when he is found bruised and beaten at the edge of his village a neighbour removes the visor and his first sortie ends as he is recognised to be the ordinary Señor Quixano. The neighbour decides to wait until it is dark before taking him home so that no one would see what a poor knight the beaten gentleman was. The neighbour recognises Don Quixote's madness but is sensitive to the need to protect his dignity. It is the simple humanity of the peasant that contrasts with the attitude of his conformist friends and family who cannot tolerate madness and react by subjecting it to contempt and ridicule.

The wounded ear in the battle with the Basque

Undaunted Don Quixote soon sets out again and in the episode of his battle with the gallant Basque he narrowly avoids death but escapes with nothing more serious than the loss of half of an ear. While Sancho dresses the bleeding ear Don Quixote discovers that his helmet has also been damaged and this turns out to be much more serious than the loss of the ear. He fears that without the helmet he will go mad and he swears that he will replace it at the earliest opportunity by defeating the next available passing knight. Sancho points out that very few knights are likely to pass along this particular road but this is brushed aside and Don Quixote decides that a barber, approaching and wearing a brass basin on his head as a sunshade, is the owner of the "Helmet of Mambrino". Again reality is represented by Sancho who claims that he sees only a man on a donkey with something shiny on his head. Don Quixote brushes this aside.

> "How can I be mistaken in what I say, unbelieving traitor?" returned Don Quixote; ...
> "that is the helmet of Mambrino", ... and without checking the fury of his charge, he cried to him: "Defend thyself, miserable being, or yield me of thine own accord that which is so reasonably my due".
> The barber, who without any expectation or apprehension of it saw this apparition coming down upon him, had no other way of saving himself from the stroke of the lance but to let himself fall off his ass; and no sooner had he touched the ground than he sprang up more nimbly than

a deer and sped away across the plain faster than the wind. He left the basin on the ground, with which Don Quixote contented himself, saying that the pagan had shown his discretion and imitated the beaver, which, finding itself pressed by the hunters, bites and cuts off with its teeth that for which, by its natural instinct, it knows it is pursued.

(Cervantes, 1605a, Vol. 1, Chapter XXI, para. 6)

Apparently, Aesop claimed (Gibbs, 2002) that, when the beaver is being chased by dogs he bites off his testicles, since he knows that this is what he is hunted for. I suspect that in a similar way it is his sanity that Don Quixote gives up as a means of survival.

When the excitement dies down the new basin is found to be incomplete and Don Quixote admits that it does seem to resemble a barber's basin. His response illustrates the ingenious way that phantasy and perception are reconciled throughout the book by invoking the action of magical enchantments deployed by his enemies.

"Look here, Sancho", said Don Quixote, "by him thou didst swear by just now I swear thou hast the most limited understanding that any squire in the world has or ever had. Is it possible that all this time thou hast been going about with me thou hast never found out that all things belonging to knights-errant seem to be illusions and nonsense and ravings, and to go always by contraries? And not because it really is so, but because there is always a swarm of enchanters in attendance upon us that change and alter everything with us, and turn things as they please, and according as they are disposed to aid or destroy us; thus what seems to thee a barber's basin seems to me Mambrino's helmet, and to another it will seem something else".

(Cervantes, 1605a, Vol. 1, Chapter XXV, para. 21)

This is another example of "I see what I want to see" and Sancho, still representing sanity but moderated by his greed, asks if he, in turn, is allowed to steal the barber's saddle and bridle. Here Don Quixote prevaricates.

"On that head I am not quite certain", answered Don Quixote, "and the matter being doubtful, pending better information, I say thou mayest change them, if so be thou hast urgent need of them".

(Cervantes, 1605a, Vol. 1, Chapter XXI, para. 28)

As in one or two other instances in his travels the knight with such high moral standards uses a sleight of hand to justify a theft. He also uses the laws of Chivalry to justify stealing the helmet and at the same time admits that he needs it to preserve his sanity. The irony is complex since he also knows that the return of what had been projected would make him sane and it is this very sanity that he believes would drive him mad.

The return of the barber whose helmet had been Stolen

The issue of what is real and what is illusion is re-opened when several chapters later, the owner of the barber's basin returns and recognising his saddle on Sancho's donkey he reclaims both the trappings and the basin. His request is denied by Don Quixote who insists that although incomplete, this is the helmet of Mambrino and not a basin. Joining in the debate Don Quixote's friends carry the joke further and pretend to agree with him that the basin is a helmet. A fracas ensues and is only resolved when the owner of the basin is bought off.

> as to Mambrino's helmet, the curate, under the rose and without Don Quixote's knowing it, paid eight reals for the basin, and the barber executed a full receipt and engagement to make no further demand then or thenceforth for evermore, amen.
>
> (Cervantes, 1605a, Vol. 1, Chapter XLVI, para. 3)

If the visor of the helmet completes the integrity of his defensive organisation we can see that the battle to sustain it was for Don Quixote one of life and death, or more immediately, sanity or madness. Paradoxically he felt that he needed his illusion if he was to stay sane and he was obliged to defy the ordinary world which threated to rob him of his illusions and force sanity on him.

The move towards sanity and death

Don Quixote's repeated efforts to sustain illusion and keep reality at bay, touch and amuse us because they are exaggerated versions of our own defensive armour sustaining our own idealised illusions. In fact his illusions do not give way for a further 75 chapters in the course of which his suffering and humiliation are enumerated in countless adventures which make no impact on his beliefs, and his devotion to his idealised good objects never wavers. Eventually, however, his confidence in his powers receives a severe blow when he is defeated in a joust by the Knight of the White Moon. Resistant to the impact of reality he falls when Sansón Carrasco, another friend from his village enters his delusional system by masquerading as a knight who topples him from his horse and obliges him to swear that he will give up knight-errantry and stay at home for a whole year.

We can imagine an infant whose love for his mother is undiminished but when he tackles his father head-on, each with lances raised, he is forced to admit defeat. We remember that he has attributed aggressive, envious attacks to the lascivious intent of others, and especially the father who threatened to wield, "the dull share of the crooked plough … to rend and pierce the tender bowels of our first mother".

Having been defeated he feels that he can no longer command admiration and he can no longer describe himself as the protector of maidens, widows, and orphans. Reality floods in and he returns home and takes to his bed as the energy that has kept him going starts to run out.

> The confession over, the curate came out saying, "Alonso Quixano the Good is indeed dying, and is indeed in his right mind; we may now go in to him while he makes his will". ... This news gave a tremendous impulse to the brimming eyes of the housekeeper, niece, and Sancho Panza his good squire, making the tears burst from their eyes and a host of sighs from their hearts; for of a truth, as has been said more than once, whether as plain Alonso Quixano the Good, or as Don Quixote of La Mancha, Don Quixote was always of a gentle disposition and kindly in all his ways, and hence he was beloved, not only by those of his own house, but by all who knew him.
>
> (Cervantes, 1605a, Vol. 1, Chapter LXXIV, para. 9)

> And then, turning to Sancho, he said, "Forgive me, my friend, that I led thee to seem as mad as myself, making thee fall into the same error I myself fell into, that there were and still are knights-errant in the world". ... "Ah!" said Sancho weeping, "don't die, master, but take my advice and live many years; for the foolishest thing a man can do in this life is to let himself die without rhyme or reason, without anybody killing him, or any hands but melancholy's making an end of him. ... Perhaps behind some bush we shall find the lady Dulcinea dis-enchanted, as fine as fine can be".
>
> "Sirs, not so fast", said Don Quixote, "'in last year's nests there are no birds this year'. I was mad, now I am in my senses; I was Don Quixote of La Mancha, I am now, as I said, Alonso Quixano the Good; and may my repentance and sincerity restore me to the esteem you used to have for me".
>
> (Cervantes, 1605a, Vol. 1, Chapter LXXIV, para. 13)

His sense of moral rightness fuelled his desire to recreate a Golden Age in which the widows and maidens, the needy and the vulnerable were treated with respect. In many of his adventures he fought not only to protect women but to insist on their rights. However he could not face the idea that his noble goals involved a denial of his own hostility. Now, after his defeat, his attempts at denial became weaker and he gave up his battle to sustain his illusions and began to face who he was.

Such was the end of the Ingenious Gentleman of La Mancha, whose village Cide Hamete would not indicate precisely, in order to leave all the towns and villages of La Mancha to contend among themselves for the right to adopt him and claim him as a son, as the seven cities of Greece contended for Homer. The lamentations of Sancho and the niece and housekeeper are omitted here, as well as the new epitaphs upon his tomb; Samson Carrasco, however, put the following lines:

> A doughty gentleman lies here;
> A stranger all his life to fear;
> ...
> A crazy man his life he passed,
> But in his senses died at last.
>
> (Cervantes, 1605a, Vol. 1,
> Chapter LXXIV, para. 19)

We are left with an immense sadness as if it was not only Don Quixote who was defeated but that the freedom to live out our own phantasies died with him.

Notes

1 Based on Steiner, J. 2020 Learning from Don Quixote. *International Journal of Psychoanalysis*, Accepted for publication.
2 The excellent modern translation of Don Quixote by Edith Grossman (Cervantes, 1605b), was used in my initial reading but for copyright reasons I am quoting from the equally excellent classical translation by John Ormsby (Cervantes, 1605a) which is surprisingly modern even though it dates from 1885.

10 Reconciling phantasy and reality
The redeeming nature of irony[1]

SONNET 138
When my love swears that she is made of truth
I do believe her, though I know she lies,
That she might think me some untutor'd youth,
Unlearned in the world's false subtleties.
Thus vainly thinking that she thinks me young,
Although she knows my days are past the best,
Simply I credit her false speaking tongue:
On both sides thus is simple truth suppress'd.
But wherefore says she not she is unjust?
And wherefore say not I that I am old?
O, love's best habit is in seeming trust,
And age in love loves not to have years told:
Therefore I lie with her and she with me,
And in our faults by lies we flatter'd be.
(Shakespeare, c. 1606)

In Shakespeare's ironic play-on-words the poet claims that his mistress pretends that he is still young and that he colludes because of his reluctance to face his ageing. "On both sides thus is simple truth suppress'd", and the outcome is a compromise with truth as the lovers profit from a denial of reality based on a kindness that allows their relationship to continue.

To me it seems that the humour in Shakespeare's sonnet is derived from an ironic acceptance of the need for illusion which at the same time recognises the reality that the illusion denies. Shakespeare understands our longing for immortality at the same time recognising it to be an illusion. Irony enables the tolerance of contradictory views and offers a smile of insight that neither view is completely true.

I believe that an ironic view helps the analyst to relate sympathetically to his patients, to his colleagues and also to himself. We believe each other even though we know we lie and sometimes the irony allows us to arrive at a deeper truth. Shakespeare's lover believed his mistress because he knew that she lied out of kindness but his idealisation of her was tempered by his suspicion that she also lied out of self-interest. He went along with the illusion knowingly and recognised that it could not be sustained indefinitely.

We are hypocrites if we pretend that we "are made of truth" and do not need illusions but we cannot casually become liars and imposters because we recognise that a respect for truth is vital for healthy relationships and necessary if we wish to foster creativity and development. An impressive feature of Shakespeare's liars is that they are sensitive to each other's feelings, and this illustrates an important quality of the ironic stance which protects us from the corruption of lying on the one hand and from the cruelty of truth on the other.

The capacity for irony is important clinically where it allows us to admit our frailty as well as that of the patient, and yet to accept that we depend on truth because lying can undermine trust. We believe our patients and yet remain sceptical, and in a similar way we have a belief in our work and remain sceptical of it. We know that both the patient and the analyst defensively distort reality to make life bearable. But we also know that there is a truth, which we strive to be aware of and respect.

Many other examples of irony can be found in Shakespeare, such as the famous advice given to his son by Polonius.

> This above all: to thine ownself be true,
> And it must follow, as the night the day,
> Thou canst not then be false to any man.
> (*Hamlet*, Act 1, Scene 3)

We begin by taking these words seriously as beautiful and truthful comments on human nature but we soon recognise that when viewed in context the words are pious and spoken by a pompous sycophantic palace official whose total disrespect for truth is evident as he spies on Hamlet and misuses his daughter in his attempt to win favour with the King. And yet the words can be seen to represent something true and I believe that their impact is deepened when they are recognised as ironic.

The same is true for some of the great scenes of reconciliation such as those so abundantly present in Shakespeare and in Mozart. For example Lear and Cordelia's happiness is deepened by the ironic knowledge that it is to be short-lived. Similarly the reconciliation between the Count and Countess in the Marriage of Figaro is based on an earnest plea for forgiveness which is deeply moving even though we know that the count's propensity for philandering is by no means over.

Jonathan Lear (2003, 2014) suggests that being human involves living up to an ideal. As an example he cites Kierkegaard who asks what it means to be a Christian and raises the equivalent question of what it means to be a psychoanalyst. Immediately we realise that when we put ourselves forward as a certain kind of person, in this case a psychoanalyst, we always fall short of what we claim to be. Inevitably self-examination gives rise to self-doubt but it also allows us to retain a respect for the endeavour without claiming it as a successful achievement. Through irony we can entertain both beliefs as does Baudelaire when he addresses his readers, *"Hypocrite lecteur mon semblable mon frere"* (1851), and we might think of a colleague or indeed a patient, "You are a hypocrite, just like me".

Irony depends on a capacity to symbolise and gives each object or event, a penumbra of meanings which collapse onto the actual object when thinking becomes concrete. Freud is said to have claimed that, "Sometimes a cigar is only a cigar", but having a rich capacity for irony he knew that it was also much more than a cigar. Irony expresses a doubt as to the truthfulness of any statement of fact and adds an element of humour that softens the severity of the truth.

I have discussed Ibsen's *The Wild Duck* (1884) in Chapter 3 and suggested that the blind pursuit of the truth was only possible because the chief characters were incapable of irony. In this chapter I will look again at Sophocles' *Oedipus the King* (5th century BC, a) to examine the importance of irony and try to show that an ironic attitude can help the reader to adopt the dual identities of participant and observer that are so necessary for the clinician.

The dramatic irony of Sophocles' Oedipus

In Chapter 3 I pointed out the parallels between the spectator of a theatrical performance and the analyst listening to the drama of his patient. I also took note of Aristotle's theory of catharsis in which the emotions of terror and pity are central to the experience of tragedy and suggested that when we feel terror we have identified with the hero of the drama and when we feel pity we have withdrawn from this identification and are observing someone we care about who is not us.

To understand a play and the effect it has on us requires that we engage in both roles, and the same is true if we want to understand our patients. In this chapter I will suggest that this dual identity as participant and observer is sustained by a capacity for irony. The two states are irreconcilable: we cannot be both involved and detached, but when we are involved there is a lingering awareness of a capacity to observe, and when we are observers we know that we have been, and again will become, involved. Because neither position is stable, this awareness leads to self-doubt, which is essential to irony and can serve as a reminder of our human frailties. Without irony, the situation can become so real that there is no gap between the play and real life, or so unreal that the drama seems to have nothing to do with us. The parallel with the psychoanalytic situation raises the possibility that we can learn something about the analytic attitude from a consideration of the impact of a theatrical performance on the audience (Schafer, 1970; Stein, 1985; Walsh, 2011).

Critics commonly use Sophocles' *Oedipus the King* (5th century BC, a) to illustrate the dramatic irony that arises when the audience observes a tragedy from a position of knowledge that is not available to the characters in the play.

For example, Fowler, in his *Dictionary of Modern English Usage* (1926), states:

> [Ironic] drama had the peculiarity of providing the double audience—one party in the secret & the other not ... All the spectators, that is, were in the secret beforehand of what would happen. But the characters, Pentheus & Oedipus & the rest, were in the dark, ... the dramatist working his effect by irony.
>
> (pp. 295–296)

I will suggest that this double attitude, one in ignorance and one in the know, reflects an internal situation in which we both know what is happening and at the same time disavow that knowledge.

Collusions to avoid reality

In *Oedipus the King* we have the classical example of a man determined to expose the truth with a single-mindedness that results in tragedy. Oedipus fails to recognise what we in the audience know and we identify with him as he gradually discovers what a disaster this exposure will be. If we emerge from our identification, however, and temporarily become sufficiently detached, we can also observe how the collusions and evasions between Oedipus and the drama's other participants led to a denial of the truth for so many years. Having triumphed over the Sphinx, Oedipus, his family, and indeed the whole city of Thebes, turned a blind eye to the facts evident to the observer and lived under an illusion of stable prosperity until a plague disturbed the status quo (Steiner, 1985).

Like the original Greek audience, we are familiar with the story, but we do not always recognise that each of the main characters had his own reasons for evading reality, and how this led them to collude in establishing and sustaining their ignorance of the facts. At the beginning of the play, Oedipus is confronted with the crisis of the plague, which leads him to embark on a quest to determine its cause. Seventeen years previously, he had entered Thebes as a homeless fugitive from the court of Corinth, to be welcomed in triumph because he had solved the riddle of the Sphinx. He was made King of Thebes in place of Laius, who had been killed a few days earlier, and accepted Jocasta, the former Queen, as his wife. However, in order to enjoy his good fortune he had to evade a number of facts that, had he pursued them, would have led him to discover the truth and to avoid the false premises on which his good fortune was based.

Moreover, the other characters in the drama—Jocasta and Creon in particular, but also the elders of the city—found it expedient *to turn a blind eye* in order to ignore events that would have enabled the truth to emerge.[2] It was this unconscious collusion that established Oedipus as an upright King and a respected father in what turned out to be an illusion of normality. Furthermore, it was an illusion that has enabled the family and the city to survive until it is shattered as the facts emerge in the course of the play.

When the tragic disillusion arrives, we in the audience are moved to terror and pity as we witness the unfolding events. In identification with Oedipus, we share in his determination to discover the truth, and we are terrified as each new discovery implicates him more certainly as the source of the corruption. However, we are also able to disidentify with the hero and observe the total situation, and this allows us to acknowledge the facts that Oedipus has been evading, as well as the complex involvements of all the characters in the cover-up. As we withdraw from the identification and stop to observe and think, we are bound to ask: "If these things can be brought to light now, why were they not discovered seventeen years ago when Oedipus first entered Thebes?"

The attitude of Oedipus

We can begin by imagining the thoughts going through the mind of Oedipus when he first entered Thebes to be acclaimed as a hero. He has left Corinth determined to avoid the prophecy at the centre of the play which ironically he proceeds to enact. He has falsely avoided his adoptive rather than his real parents and without compunction has killed an older man with a royal retinue. He has married the widow of the King, a woman old enough to be his mother, and he did this within a very short time of being told by the oracle that he was destined to kill his father and marry his mother.

We know the fateful history, but we watch attentively as it becomes clear that Oedipus failed to make the crucial connections. The city must have been buzzing with news of the recent murder of King Laius, but Oedipus had not asked where the King had been killed, by whom he was attended, or what he looked like. Instead of pursuing the obvious inquiries, Oedipus has erected a plausible facade to cover up the truth, which he persuaded himself and others to accept. He felt safe in Thebes because he convinced himself that the one thing he feared was a return to Corinth, where he might kill King Polybus and marry Merope, the couple he believed to be his parents. He overlooked the fact that he had gone to Delphi expressly to ask about his parentage because doubts had been cast on it, and the oracle had failed to reassure him. He accepted his new situation without a qualm because, as Green (1987) suggested, the desire to enjoy Laius's throne and Jocasta's bed made him a poor logician.

The testimony of Teiresias

One of the remarkable moments of the play occurs quite near the beginning when Oedipus swears to find and banish the killer of Laius, and the ancient soothsayer Teiresias is sent for. At first he refuses to identify the guilty man, but when Oedipus becomes childishly abusive, Teiresias gets angry and tells him in plain terms first that the killer Oedipus is seeking is *himself* and then that it is *he* who is "the cursed polluter of this land ... living in sinful union with the one you love" (Watling, 1947, p. 36).

Creon, the elders, and Oedipus all hear this, and all go on to act as if they have not heard it. The remarkable thing is that we in the audience also hear it and, while knowing it to be true and witnessing the wholesale denial, we identify with Oedipus and join in the collusion, apprehensively waiting for the denouement as the play gradually and with many diversions leads inexorably toward the truth.

Jocasta's attitude

Jocasta must have been told of the death of her husband, and she knew of the prediction that led him to fear that his son would murder him. Despite this she agreed to the marriage and repeatedly expressed her contempt of prophecy. In the play, she reassures Oedipus by insisting that guilt is inappropriate because all lives are ruled by chance. Marriage to the youthful Oedipus offered her the opportunity to remain Queen of Thebes and once again to bear children. It is not difficult to suppose that these advantages led her to turn a blind eye to the truth and to collude in the cover-up.

As psychoanalysts, we recognise that the oedipal illusion is universal and includes a phantasy of mutual love between mother and child, irrespective of differences in age. Jocasta's fate, however, reminds us of the tragic consequences if these illusions remain untouched by reality.

Creon's attitude

Jocasta's brother, Creon, was responsible for ruling the city after Laius was killed. He explains that he had no ambition to rule and was content to retain an influence in the background. He shows no surprise when told of Teiresias's accusations, despite their terrible import, saying only "If he did so, you know best" (Watling, 1947, p. 40). Earlier when Oedipus asks what stopped them from tracking down the King's killer there and then, Creon replies, "The Sphinx with her riddles forced us to turn our attention from insoluble mysteries to more immediate matters" (Watling, 1947, p. 29).

Oedipus asks why Teiresias was not summoned to identify the murderer at that time, only to be told that he *had been* summoned but had remained silent. When Oedipus asks why he has now spoken after staying silent for so long, Creon answers simply, "I do not presume to say more than

I know" (Watling, 1947, p. 41). It makes sense for Creon to deny his complicity; Oedipus cannot be saved, but Creon can—and in fact he comes out of the drama unscathed.

The attitude of the elders

Finally, the chorus of elders, on stage throughout the unfolding of the drama, are shown to be concerned with their own interests as they begin to suspect that all is not well with the King. When Oedipus proclaims that he will find the guilty party, they deny having had anything to do with it and indicate they prefer divine knowledge to that arrived at by investigating reality.

Even though the elders heard Teiresias make clear that it is Oedipus who is the killer of Laius and the polluter of the land, they speak of an unknown robber with blood-stained hands who has committed the most unspeakable of unspeakable crimes, and refer to him roaming the countryside at large. Eventually, they admit that Teiresias's testimony is disturbing, but they affirm their compliance and decline to take sides. They are terrified of the chaos that they think will arise if their King is dethroned, and they are also playing it safe while there is a chance that he might survive.

The cover-up

A cover-up requires conspirators who agree either overtly or tacitly to collaborate. If Creon had called for a proper inquiry, the witness would have been interrogated and the truth would have come out. If Jocasta had not ignored the oracle that she so hated, she might not have turned a blind eye to her young husband's resemblance to Laius, to the fact that his age was precisely that of her son had he lived, or to the scars on his feet that must have puzzled her. If the elders, too, had been more vigilant and not so concerned about backing the winning party, they might have demanded an inquiry, or at least asked about their new King's background.

The cover-up could only take place because it suited several parties at the same time, and thus enabled the participants to be of mutual service to each other. We in the audience also collude in the cover-up because we empathically identify with everyone's need to do so.

Oedipus's remarkable pursuit of truth and the horrible denouement

If we recognise the only-too-human evasions of truth that led to the massive cover-up in *Oedipus the King*, then the determination and courage shown by Oedipus as he faces reality is even more remarkable. We see him vacillating and struggling with his ambivalence, but this only makes his final achievement more impressive.

The climax of the play occurs when the shepherd who took Oedipus away as a baby makes the whole truth clear, and Oedipus accepts it with great courage and without prevarication or excuse. He admits everything, saying simply, "Alas, all out! All is known! No more concealment! Oh light! May I never look on you again, revealed as I am, sinful in my begetting, sinful in marriage, sinful in the shedding of blood" (Watling, 1947, p. 56).

At this point, the truth, although awful, seems to be accepted by Oedipus, but the next event in the tragedy—the final blow of Jocasta's death—seems to make the situation unbearable. A messenger announces the suicide of the Queen and describes what happens next: when Oedipus sees her suspended body, he cuts her down and then puts out his own eyes with her brooches. We are moved with horror and pity as we recognise that his guilt has led to this tragic self-mutilation, which points to the possibility that looking at the truth became impossible when it included responsibility for Jocasta's death. The murder of his father and the marriage to his mother were part of the prophecy, but the Queen's death was unexpected and doubly shocking. Nowhere was Oedipus warned that his crime would devastate and destroy his mother as well.

Moreover, the hero is now alone, with neither parent able to serve as a good object to make tragedy and guilt more bearable. After his determined pursuit of the truth and his courageous acceptance of responsibility, his self-blinding initiates a move away from truth, and the evasion deepens in *Oedipus at Colonus* (Sophocles, 5th century BC, b), where Oedipus adopts a God-like status and emphatically denies his guilt (Steiner, 1990, 1993).

Sophocles highlights the conflict between the wish to face the truth and the wish to evade it, surely one of the deepest of human conflicts, and one that every patient who embarks on an analysis has to wrestle with. We can identify with the hero who espouses such devotion to truth, but I believe that looking again at *Oedipus* can lead us to temper our love for truth with a recognition of its cruelty and an acceptance of the need for evasions that can make life bearable. This means that the acceptance of reality is more complex than a simple facing of facts, and that different visions of reality are required to enrich our understanding and to make it more true. To support the patient as he embarks on developments in accord with reality requires the analyst to appreciate how complex, multi-layered, and rich our relationship with reality is. The analyst needs to accept that reality can be cruel, that evasions and illusions are universal, and that understanding them is often only possible in a wider context, where the total situation can be taken into account.

Comic, romantic, tragic, and ironic visions of reality

I have used *Oedipus the King* to argue that the discovery and acceptance of reality is complex, and that the history, circumstances, and personalities of the participants must be taken into account to gain a broader and truer view of the total situation. In an important contribution, Schafer (1970) explored some of these complexities and put forward the view that the apperception of reality depends on the attitude and state of mind of the perceiver. He considers four different attitudes to reality, which he discusses under the headings of the *comic, romantic, tragic,* and *ironic* visions. His thinking is based in literary criticism (Frye, 1957), and these visions have a relevance beyond the psychoanalytic setting, dealing as they do with basic human understanding and the definition of what it means to be human (Lear, 2003, 2014). The relevance for the psychoanalyst is partly that these visions may help him better recognise attitudes and states of mind in his patients, but also that they may lead him to a clearer view of his own approach to reality.

Schafer's *comic* and *romantic* visions have much in common with the journey of the hero described in Chapter 4, in which a hero is driven to recover an idealised state and to achieve the desired outcome by overcoming obstacles, rather than by trying to understand them. In this sense, these two visions support illusion and invoke the pursuit of success rather than the acceptance of truth. In analysis, they can be thought of as antithetical to truth, and yet they play an important role in enhancing the patient's quality of life and they contribute to a liveliness that adds to the pleasures of living. Eventually, when attempts are made to face reality, a critical issue is whether or not the resultant experience of disillusion is bearable.

In contrast to the optimism of the comic and romantic visions, the *tragic* vision involves an acceptance of reality and a suffering of both the pain and the pleasures that reality bestows. The tragic vision gives depth to experience and makes a simplistic goal of avoidance of pain seem superficial. To give an example, Klein described how a deeper and more enduring meaning of love can arise only after we have suffered the pain and depression that follow attacks on our good objects (Klein, 2017). We do not fully appreciate people or things that we value until we face their loss. The central role of loss in tragedy can remind us of the importance of time and the reality of death and it is in tragedy above all that time makes its presence felt. Perhaps most significant is the fact that the tragic vision moves us because it describes the often catastrophic meeting of evasions of reality when confronted by the truth. This means that the terrible pain and disappointment of the loss of idealised phantasies is part of the tragic vision and is, I think, an essential feature of it (Steiner, 2013, 2015).

It seems to me that in both *The Wild Duck* and in *Oedipus the King*, it is drama of disillusionment that gives the tragedy its bite. We witness how the people who have come to matter to us are crushed by the impact of reality, and we are moved to feel terror and pity that enriches our lives.

The ironic vision

A consideration of the tragic vision helps us to recognise that a gap has emerged between the protagonist in the throes of relinquishment of his illusion and the audience aware of the reality he has so energetically been avoiding. Moreover, this gap exists in all of us as we alternate between participation and observation in the dramas of others, but also in our own dramas, which we both live through and reflect on. The *ironic* vision involves an awareness of this gap and a willingness to tolerate both points of view. We realise that all along we have known something of the truth; we feel pity for the blindness of the protagonists, and we shudder as collusions and seductions are exposed.

Because these attitudes are contradictory, they cannot be resolved, and the conflict has to be recognised as inevitable and permanent. It is part of the human condition that we wish both to deny and to accept reality. I think it is a sense of irony that allows us to live with this contradiction and also with other contradictions, such as that between subjective and objective, symbolic and concrete, actual and ideal.

The subjective and the objective

Lear (2003, 2014) also suggests that irony has an importance in the relationship between subjective and objective knowledge especially in relation to the psychoanalytic attitude. If we consider the subjective to arise from an experiencing self, we can link it with the feelings and thoughts that we have as we participate in our own or in other people's dramas. The objective view, by contrast, arises from our position as observer, self-reflective in our own dramas and experiencing those of others from the outside. The fact that we are human beings means that neither the position of the involved participant nor that of the detached observer is stable, and we alternate between them as we are pulled into and out of either position.

Sometimes the detached position as an observer is thought to be scientific and is pursued in attempts to make psychoanalysis respectable. Such attempts are valuable and important, but only if they are tempered by an ironic vision that recognises that we can only transiently extricate ourselves from subjective involvement. This does not mean that objectivity is impossible, but rather that it is always suspect and open to self-doubt. An ironic view that recognises the value of both the subjective and the objective can in this sense be more truthful than a simplistic objectivity.

Since it aims at detachment, irony may be used defensively to lessen the impact of tragedy. Fowler (1926) speaks of the delight of irony in a "secret intimacy" (p. 296) with those in the know, and it is these delights that may lead to feelings of superiority as we disengage from the tragedy and look down on those suffering it. This relief may contribute to the humorous element in irony, which causes us to smile as we see the discrepancy between the tragic struggles of the protagonists on stage and our own apparently deeper knowledge. Irony may then descend into sarcasm and mockery if self-observation gives way to condescension. The distinction is important; in true irony, the smile is always tinged with pain since we are simultaneously laughing at ourselves and identifying with the protagonists of the tragedy.

It seems to me that the ironic view allows us to appreciate the importance of both sides in the conflict between reality and illusion. It encompasses both the comic and the tragic, the subjective and the objective, the concrete and the symbolic. If we are able to experience each of these states in turn, we can become aware of the conflict and contradictions in our complex relationship with reality. We can also recognise how easily the ironic view can collapse into a concrete certainty with the potential for insensitivity and cruelty.

The collapse of irony and the creation of the concrete

When the analyst is under pressure from the concrete projections of his patient his own capacity to use symbols is interfered with. This is most extreme in the case of psychotic patients but lesser forms of such symbolic paralysis are common. Building on Segal's studies of symbolic function (Segal, 1954), Bion (1959, 1962) proposed that sometimes the capacity to symbolise is lost and that concrete objects are used in place of thoughts. These concrete objects cannot be used for thinking or dreaming and can only be dealt with by projective identification.

P. C. Sandler (1997) has extended Bion's model and proposed that when symbols give rise to unbearable anxiety an anti-symbolic process comes into operation to transform symbolic elements back into concrete objects.[3] It seems to me possible that the inverse is also true, namely, that in order to deploy projective identification concrete elements are necessary. When the patient's symbolic function is intact, meaningful connections are made to thoughts, memories, dreams, and other resonances in his life and it is partly because of these connections that symbolic entities are difficult to get rid of by projective identification. They are also less potent in their effect on the analyst's mind than are their concrete counterparts. According to this idea abstract symbolic elements have first to be converted back into a concrete form in order that they can be got rid of by evacuation through projective identification.

I think it is likely that this type of reversal of symbolic capacity is an active process which operates widely and which can also be used defensively by the analyst when he finds that he is unable to tolerate the symbolic implications of what has been projected into him. The adoption of an analytic stance may then create too much anxiety and guilt for it to be sustained, and concrete thinking becomes necessary for the analyst just as it was for the patient. Most of the time the analyst is trying to deal with the patient's projections, whether concrete or not, by containing and understanding them and for this he has to be able to deploy his symbolic capacities. However sometimes he may be driven by the experiences evoked in him to reverse his capacity to symbolise in order to transform the experience back into a concrete projectable form.

Usually this takes place at an unconscious level and the projection takes the form of an enactment disguised as an interpretation. These interpretive enactments (Joseph, 2003; Steiner, 2006a) subsequently makes the analyst feel guilty and make it very difficult for him to recognise what is happening and hence it may become difficult for him to extricate himself from inter-actions in which both analyst and patient use projective identification of a concrete kind. At these times the analyst's level of thinking seems to be no different to that of the patient.

From a broader point of view we can see that the reversal of symbolic capacity is a necessary mechanism to relieve the individual of unbearable mental experiences, whether he is a patient or an analyst. Without it pro-jective identification would be impossible and our defensive organisation would not be able to function. If the analyst can resist some of the pressure to enact and retain a capacity to think, he may be able to recognise a meaningful communication underlying the projections. He may then become aware of the patient's need to project and be in a position to help the patient to feel understood. An ironic stance can help the analyst to rec-ognise and tolerate the patient's concrete thinking as well as his own.

In her lectures on technique, Klein suggests that a good analytic attitude involves a

> rather curious state of mind, eager and at the same time patient, detached from its subject and at the same time fully absorbed in it. [This requires a] balance between different and partly conflicting ten-dencies and psychological drives, and ... a good co-operation between several different parts of our mind.
>
> (Klein, 2017, p. 30)

These characteristics seem to me to be part of an ironic stance that enables us to be fully absorbed in the patient's narrative and also detached from it, for partly conflicting attitudes to co-exist and for different parts of the mind to co-operate. When we are functioning well we can allow an eager involve-ment with our patients without becoming dangerously over-involved with them and to observe with a detached scepticism without the adoption of a position of superiority.

Notes

1 Based on Steiner, J. (2016) Illusion, Disillusion, and Irony in Psychoanalysis. *Psy-choanalytic Quarterly*, 85:427–447.
2 In an earlier paper (Steiner, 1985) I use the term *to turn a blind eye* to denote a situation in which we have access to reality but choose to ignore it because it proves convenient to do so. This mechanism involves a degree of ambiguity as to how conscious or unconscious the knowledge is; most often, we are vaguely aware that we are choosing not to look at the facts, but without being conscious of what it is we are evading. These views of Sophocles' play are based on the

work of Philip Vellacott, an idiosyncratic classicist who is known for his translations of Aeschylus and Euripides but whose views on Oedipus (Vellacott, 1971) have not been generally accepted.

3 Bion uses a particular nomenclature which some analysts find useful. He refers to the concrete symbols, as beta-elements and to the transformational process as alpha-function. The symbols proper are called alpha elements and are, "suitable for employment in dream thoughts, unconscious waking thinking, contact barrier, memory. By contrast, beta-elements are the undigested sense impressions, indistinguishable from the thing in itself to which the sense-impression corresponds. These are employed for hallucination and projective identification" (p. 26). Sandler describes the reversal of symbolic function to result from an anti-alpha function.

References

Abrams, M. H. (1956). *A Glossary of Literary Terms.* New York: Holt, Rinehart, and Winston (7th Edition, 1999).

Akhtar, S. (1996). "Someday" and "If Only" Fantasies: Pathological Optimism and Inordinate Nostalgia as Related Forms of Idealization. *J. Am. Psychoanal. Assn.*, 44: 723–753.

Anthi, P. R. (1990). Freud's Dream in *Norekdal* Style. *Scandinavian Psychoanal. Rev.*, 13: 138–160.

Balsam, R. (2013). Freud, Females, Childbirth, and Dissidence: Margarete Hilferding, Karen Horney, and Otto Rank. *Psychoanal. Rev.*, 100(5): 695–716.

Bate, W. J. (1945). The sympathetic imagination in Eighteenth-century English criticism. *J. Engl. Lit. Hist.*, 12: 144–164.

Beer, A. (2008). *Milton, Poet, Pamphleteer, and Patriot.* London: Bloomsbury.

Beres, D. and Arlow, J. A. (1974). Fantasy and Identification in Empathy. *Psychoanal. Quart.*, 43: 15–181.

Bion, W. R. (1959). Attacks on Linking. *Int. J. Psycho-Anal.*, 40: 308–315 (Reprinted in *Second Thoughts*, pp. 93–109, London: Heinemann (1967)).

Bion, W. R. (1962). *Learning from Experience.* London: Heinemann.

Bion, W. R. (1970). *Attention and Interpretation.* London: Tavistock.

Birksted-Breen, D. (1993). *The Gender Conundrum.* London: Routledge.

Birksted-Breen, D. (1996). Phallus, Penis and Mental Space. *Int. J. Psychoanal.*, 61: 39–52.

Blake, W. (1825–27). The Marriage of Heaven and Hell Reproduced. In *Facsimile*, ed. M. Plowman. London and Toronto: J.M. Dent & Sons, 1927.

Bloom, H. (1975). Milton and His Precursors. In *Paradise Lost. An Authoritative Text, Backgrounds and Sources Criticism*, ed. S. Elledge. New York: Norton, pp. 555–568.

Bolognini, S. (1997). Empathy and 'Empathism'. *Int. J. Psycho-Anal.*, 78: 279–293.

Britton, R. (2004). Subjectivity, Objectivity, and Triangular Space. *Psychoanal. Q.*, 73: 47–61.

Britton, R. S. (2003). The Female Castration Complex: Freud's Big Mistake? Chapter 4. In *Sex, Death and the Super-Ego*, London: Karnac, pp. 57–71.

Bunnin, N. and Yu, J. (2004). *Blackwell Dictionary of Western Philosophy.* Oxford: Blackwell Publishing.

Campbell, J. (1949). *The Hero with a Thousand Faces.* Novato, CA: New World Library.

Cervantes, M. (1605a) *The History of Don Quixote*, Translated by John Ormsby (1885): Project Gutenberg. Release Date: July 27, 2004 [EBook #996]. http://www.gutenberg.org/files/996/996-h/996-h.htm.

Cervantes, M. (1605b). *Don Quixote*, trans. by Edith Grossman. London: Vintage Books, Random House 2005 (Kindle Edition).

Chasseguet-Smirgel, J. (1976). Freud and Female Sexuality—The Consideration of Some Blind Spots in the Exploration of the 'Dark Continent. *Int. J. Psycho-Anal.*, 57: 275–286.

Coates, S. W. (2016). Can Babies Remember Trauma? Symbolic Forms of Representation in Traumatized Infants. *J. Am. Psychoanal. Assn.*, 64: 751–776.

Davies, R. (2012). Anxiety: The Importunate Companion. Psychoanalytic Theory of Castration and Separation Anxieties and Implications for Clinical Technique. *Int. J. Psycho-Anal.*, 93(5): 1101–1114.

Deutsch, H. (1925). The Psychology of Women in Relation to the Functions of Reproduction1. *Int. J. Psycho-Anal.*, 6: 405–418.

Devereux, G. (1953). Why Oedipus Killed Laius—A Note on the Complementary Oedipus Complex in Greek Drama. *Int. J. Psycho-Anal.*, 34: 132–141.

Dimen, M. (1997). The Engagement between Psychoanalysis and Feminism. *Contemp. Psychoanal.*, 33: 527–548.

Dostoevsky, F. (1868) Letter from Geneva to his Favorite Young Niece, Sophia Ivanova. January 13, 1868. Quoted by Loseff L (1998) Dostoevsky & 'Don Quixote'. New York Review of Books. Vol. 45, November 19 Issue, 1998.

Edmunds, L. and Ingber, R. (1977). Psychoanalytical Writings on the Oedipus Legend: A Bibliography. *Am. Imago*, 34: 374–386.

Eliot, G. (1876). *Daniel Deronda*. London: Penguin Books, Chapter 11, p. 160 (1967).

Elledge, S. (1975). *Paradise Lost. An Authoritative Text, Backgrounds and Sources Criticism*. New York: Norton.

Empson, W. (1965). *Milton's God*. New York: Norton (Extracts reprinted in Elledge S. (1975) *Paradise Lost. An Authoritative Text, Backgrounds and Sources Criticism*).

Feldman, M. (1994). Projective Identification in Phantasy and Enactment. *Psychoanal. Inq.*, 14: 423–440.

Feldman, M. (2000). Some Views on the Manifestation of the Death Instinct in Clinical Work. *Int. J. Psycho-Anal.*, 81: 53–65.

Ferenczi, S. (1913). Stages in the Development of the Sense of Reality. In *First Contributions to Psychoanalysis*. London: Hogarth Press, pp. 213–240 (1952).

Fish, S. (1967). *Surprised by Sin: The Reader in Paradise Lost*. Cambridge, MA: Harvard University Press (2nd Edition, 1998).

Fish, S. (1975). *Discovery as Form in Paradise Lost*. New York: Norton, pp. 526–536 (Extracts reprinted in Elledge S. (1975) *Paradise Lost. An authoritative Text, Backgrounds and Sources Criticism*).

Forster, E. M. (1924). *A Passage to India*. London: Edward Arnold.

Forster, E. M. (1936). Ibsen the Romantic. In *The Wild Duck*, ed. H. Ibsen and trans. by D. B. Christiani. New York: Norton, pp. 143–146 (1968).

Fowler, H. W. (1926). *A Dictionary of Modern English Usage*. Oxford: Clarendon Press, 1937.

Freud, S. (1897) Letter 69. Extracts from the Fliess Papers. *S E*, 1: 259–260 (I no longer believe in my neurotica).

Freud, S. (1900). The Interpretation of Dreams. The Standard Edition of the Complete Psychological Works of Sigmund Freud, Volume IV (1900): The Interpretation of Dreams (First Part), ix–627.

Freud, S. (1906). Psychopathic Characters on the Stage (1942 [1905 or 1906]). *The Standard Edition of the Complete Psychological Works of Sigmund Freud*, VII: 1901–1905, 303–310.

Freud, S. (1908). Creative Writers and Day-dreaming. *S E*, 9: 143–153.

Freud, S. (1911). Formulation on the Two Principles of Mental Functioning. *S E*, 12: 215–226.

Freud, S. (1914) On Narcissism: An Introduction. *S E*, 14: 73–102.

Freud, S. (1916). On Transience. *S E*, 14: 305–307.

Freud, S. (1917) Introductory Lectures on Psycho-analysis. *S E*, 16 Chapter XX1, The development of the libido and the sexual organisation. 320–338.

Freud, S. (1919). 'A Child is being Beaten', A Contribution to the Study of Sexual Perversions. *S E*, 17: 175–204.

Freud, S. (1923). The Ego and the Id. *S E*, 19: 13–66.

Freud, S. (1924). Neurosis and Psychosis. *S E*, 19: 149–153.

Freud, S. (1927). Fetishism. *S E*, 21: 149–157.

Freud, S. (1930). Civilisation and Its Discontents. *S E*, 21: 59–145.

Freud, S. (1937). Analysis Terminable and Interminable. *S E*, 23: 211–253.

Freud, S. (1938). Splitting of the Ego in the Process of Defence. The Standard Edition of the Complete Psychological Works of Sigmund Freud, Volume XXIII (1937–1939): Moses and Monotheism. *An Outline of Psycho-Analysis and Other Works*, 271–278.

Freud, S. (1941). Having and Being in Children, p. 299. July 12, 1938. *In Findings, Ideas, Problems. S E*, 23: 299–300.

Frye, N. (1957). *Anatomy of Criticism*. New York: Athaneum, 1967.

Fulmer, R. H. (2006). From Law to Love: Young Adulthood in Milton's Paradise Lost. *Am. Imago*, 63: 25–56.

Gabbard, G O (1993). On Hate in Love Relationships: The Narcissism of Minor Differences Revisited. *Psychoanal. Q.*, 62: 229–238.

Gibbs, L. (2002). *Aesop's Fables*, A new translation. Oxford University Press (World's Classics).

Goldner, V. (2000). Reading and Writing, Talking and Listening. *Stud. Gend. Sex*, 1: 1–7.

Graves, R. (1955). *Greek Myths*. London: Penguin, Oedipus Story, p. 219.

Green, A. (1986) 'The Dead Mother' Chapter 7. In *'On Private Madness'*. Karnac, pp. 142–173.

Green, A. (1987). Oedipus, Freud, and Us. In *Psychoanalytic Approaches to Literature and Film*, eds. M. Charney, J. Reppen and J. A. Flieger.London/Toronto: Associated Press, pp. 215–237.

Hanly, C. (1984). Ego Ideal and Ideal Ego. *Int. J. Psycho-Anal.*, 65: 253–261.

Hawking, S. (1996). The Beginning of Time. www.hawking.org.uk/lectures.html

Hesiod. (2007). (7th Century BC). *Hesiod the Homeric Hymns and Homerica*, trans. by Hugh G. Evelyn-White. Charleston, SC: BiblioLife.

Hodges, H. A. (1944) Wilhelm Dilthey: An Introduction (International Library of Sociology and Social Reconstruction).

Holmes, R. (1995). *Footsteps: The Adventures of a Romantic Biographer*. London: Harpers.

Horney, K. (1924). On the Genesis of the Castration Complex in Women. *Int. J. Psychoanal.*, 5: 50–65.

Horney, K. (1926). The Flight from Womanhood: The Masculinity-Complex in Women, as Viewed by Men and by Women. *Int. J. Psycho-Anal.*, 7: 324–339.

Ibsen, H. (1879). *A Doll's House*. Clayton, DE: Prestwick House. 2005.

Ibsen, H. (1884). *The Wild Duck*, trans. by D. B. Christiani. New York: Norton, 1968.

Joseph, B. (2003). Ethics and Enactment. *Psycho-Anal. Eur.*, 57: 147–153.

Keats, J. (1819). Ode to a Nightingale. www.poetryfoundation.org/poems/44479/ode-to-a-nightingale

Klein, M. (1932). Chapter III An Obsessional Neurosis in a Six-Year-Old Girl. In *The Psycho-Analysis of Children*, pp. 35–57. Reprinted in *The Writings of Melanie Klein*. 2 London: The Hogarth Press. (1975).

Klein, M. (1940). Mourning and its Relation to Manic-depressive States. *Int. J Psycho-Anal.*, 21: 125–153 (Reprinted in *The Writings of Melanie Klein*, 1, 344–369. London: The Hogarth Press. (1975)).

Klein, M. (1957). *Envy and Gratitude*. London: Tavistock (Reprinted in *The Writings of Melanie Klein*, 3, 176–235, London: Hogarth Press,1975).

Klein, M. (1963). On the Sense of Loneliness. Chapter 16. In *Envy and Gratitude and Other Works 1946–1963*. London: The Hogarth Press and the Institute of Psycho-Analysis, pp. 300–317 (*Int. Psycho-Anal. Lib.*, 104, 1–346 (1975).

Klein, M. (2017). *Melanie Klein's Lectures on Technique (1936): Their Relevance for Contemporary Psychoanalysis. Including Transcripts of Her Seminars of 1952*, Edited with critical review by J. Steiner. Routledge.

Lear, J. (2003). *Therapeutic Action: An Earnest Plea for Irony*. London: Karnac Books.

Lear, J. (2014). *A Case for Irony (Tanner Lectures on Human Values)*. Cambridge, MA: Harvard University Press.

Loewald, H. W. (1962). The Superego and the Ego-Ideal. *Int. J. Psycho-Anal.*, 43: 264–268.

Loseff, L. (1998) Dostoevsky & 'Don Quixote'. New York Review of Books. Vol. 45, November 19 Issue, 1998.

Mahler, M., Pine, F., and Bergman, A. (1975). The Psychological Birth of the Human Infant. New York: Basic Books.

Mahler, M. S. (1972). Rapprochement Subphase of the Separation-Individuation Process. *Psychoanal. Q.*, 41: 487–506.

Mahler, M. S. (1974). Symbiosis and Individuation—The Psychological Birth of the Human Infant. *Psychoanal. St. Child*, 29: 89–106.

Makari, G. J. (1998). The Seductions of History: Sexual Trauma in Freud's Theory and Historiography. *Int. J. Psycho-Anal.*, 79: 857–869.

Masson, J. M. (1984). *The Assault on Truth*. New York: Straus & Giroux.

Meltzer, D. (1966). The Relation of Anal Masturbation to Projective Identification. *Int. J Psycho-Anal.*, 47: 335–342.

Milton, J. (1674) Paradise Lost. From Luxon, Thomas H., ed. The Milton Reading Room, www.dartmouth.edu/~milton, March, 2008.

Mitchell, J. (2013). Siblings. *Psychoanal. St. Child*, 67: 14–34.

Money-Kyrle, R. (1968). Cognitive Development. *Int. J Psycho-Anal.*, 49: 691–698 (Reprinted in *The Collected Papers of Roger Money-Kyrle*. 416–433, Perthshire: Clunie Press(1978)).

Money-Kyrle, R. (1971). The Aim of Psycho-analysis. *Int. J. Psycho-Anal.*, 52: 103–106 (Reprinted in *The Collected Papers of Roger Money-Kyrle*. 442–449, Perthshire: Clunie Press(1978)).

Muecke, D. C. (1970). *Irony*. London: Methuen.

Murray, L. and Trevarthen, C. (1985). Emotional Regulation of Interactions between Two-month-olds and Their Mothers. In *Social Perception in Infants*, eds. T. M. Field and N. A. Fox.Norwood, NJ: Ablex, pp. 177–198.

Nabokov, V. (1984). Six Lectures on *Don Quixote*, ed. F. Bowers. Jovanovich, NY: Harcourt, Brace.

Nagel, T. (1974). What is It Like to Be a Bat? *The Philosophical Review*, 83: 435–450.

Person, E. S. and Ovesey, L. (1983). Psychoanalytic Theories of Gender Identity. *J. Am. Acad. Psychoanal. Dyn. Psychiatr.*, 11(2): 203–226.

Pine, F. (1980). On the Expansion of the Affect Array: A Developmental Description. In *Rapprochement: The Critical Subphase of Separation-Individuation*, eds. R. Lax, S. Bach, & J. A. Burland. New York: Jason Aronson, pp. 217–233.

Racker, H. (1957) The Meaning and Uses of Countertransference. *Psycho-anal. Quart.*, 26: 303–357. Reprinted in *Transference and Countertransference*. London: Hogarth. (1968).

Ricks, C. (1963). *Milton's Grand Style* New York: Norton, pp. 537–554 (Extracts reprinted in Elledge S. (1975) Paradise Lost. An authoritative Text, Backgrounds and Sources Criticism).

Riviere, J. (1929). Womanliness as a Masquerade. *Int. J. Psycho-Anal.*, 10: 303–313.

Rosenfeld, H. A. (1971). Contributions to the Psychopathology of Psychotic Patients. The Importance of Projective Identification in the Ego Structure and Object Relations of the Psychotic Patient. In *Problems of Psychosis*, eds. P. Doucet and C. Laurin. Amsterdam: Excerpta Medica, pp. 115–128 (Reprinted in Spillius E. Bott (1988) *Melanie Klein Today. 1. Mainly Theory*. London: Routledge, pp. 117–137, and in Steiner J (2008) *Rosenfeld in Retrospect: Some Essays on his Clinical Influence*. Steiner J (Ed). Routledge).

Rudat, W. E. (1985). Milton's Paradise Lost: Augustinian Theology and Fantasy. *Am. Imago*, 42: 297–313.

Rudnytsky, P. L. (1988). "Here Only Weak"; Sexuality and the Structure of Trauma in Paradise Lost. *Psychoanal. Rev.*, 75: 153–176.

Coleridge, S. T. (1810). *Lectures on Shakespeare*. London: J.M. Dent and Sons. 1936.

Sandler, P. C. (1997). The Apprehension of Psychic Reality: Extensions of Bion's Theory of Alpha-Function. *Int. J. Psycho-Anal.*, 78: 43–52.

Schafer, R. (1970). The Psychoanalytic Vision of Reality. *Int. J. Psycho-Anal.*, 51: 279–297.

Schiller, F. (1795). *Über naive und sentimentalische Dichtung*, ed. S. Werke. Stuttgart: Cotta (1838).

Schore, A. N. (1991). Early Superego Development. *Psychoanal. Contemp. Thought*, 14: 187–250.

Segal, H. (1952). A Psycho-analytical Approach to Aesthetics. *Int. J. Psychoanal*, 33: 196–207 (Reprinted in *The Work of Hanna Segal*, New York: Jason Aronson. (1981), pp. 185–206).

Segal, H. (1954). A Note on Schizoid Mechanisms Underlying Phobia Formation. *Int. J. Psycho-Anal.*, 35: 238–441 (Reprinted in *The Work of Hanna Segal*, pp. 137–144. New York: Jason Aronson (1981)).

Segal, H. (1957). Notes on Symbol Formation. *Int. J. Psycho-anal.*, 38: 391–397 (Reprinted in *The Work of Hanna Segal*. New York: Jason Aronson (1981), pp. 49–65).

Segal, H. (1972). A Delusional System as a Defence against the Re-emergence of a Catastrophic Situation. *Int. J Psycho-Anal.*, 53: 393–401.

Segal, H. (1994). Phantasy and Reality. *Int. J Psycho-anal*, 75: 359–401 (Reprinted in *Psychoanalysis, Literature and War: Papers 1972–1995* (1997), London: Routledge).

Segal, H. (2007). Disillusionment: The Story of Adam and Eve and that of Lucifer. In *Yesterday, Today, and Tomorrow*. London: Routledge, pp. 25–36.

Shakespeare, W. (1592–1594). Richard lll, Act 1 Scene 1. http://shakespeare.mit.edu/richardiii/full.html

Shakespeare, W. (circa 1600). Hamlet, Act 1. *Scene III, l.564* www.opensourceshake speare.org/views/plays/play_view.php?WorkID=hamlet&Act=1&Scene=3&Scope=scene

Shakespeare, W. (circa 1606). The Sonnets. www.shakespeares-sonnets.com/sonnet/138

Shelley, P. B. (1821). A Defence of Poetry. In *Essays, Letters from Abroad, Translations and Fragments*, ed. E. Moxon. London (1840). https://smile.amazon.co.uk/Essays-Letters-Abroad-Translations-Fragments-ebook/dp/B07NNZNG95/ref=sr_1_1?key words=Shelley%2C+Essays%2C+Letters+from+Abroad%2C+Translations+and +Fragments&qid=1582651406&sr=8-1

Smith, A. (1759). Theory of Moral Sentiments. https://oll.libertyfund.org/titles/theory-of-moral-sentiments-and-essays-on-philosophical-subjects

Sodre, I. (2004). Who's Who? Notes on Pathological Identifications. In *Pursuit of Psychic Change*, eds. E. Hargreaves and A. Varchevker. London: Routledge, pp. 53–65 (New Library of Psychoanalysis, p. 206).

Sodre, I. (2008). "Even Now, now, Very Now": On Envy and the Hatred of Love. Chapter XIV. In *Envy and Gratitude Revisited*, eds. P. Roth and A. Lemma. International Psychoanalytical Association, pp. 19–34.

Sodre, I. (2012). Personal Communication.

Sodre, I. (2013) 'For Ever Wilt Thou Love, and She Be Fair!' On Quixotism and the Golden Age of Pre-Genital Sexuality. Chapter VII. In *Imaginary Existences: Dream Daydream Phantasy Fiction*, ed. P. Roth, pp. 105–120.

Sodre, I. (2017) Suddenly The Window Opened. Unpublished Paper.

Sophocles. (1982). (5th century b.c.). *Oedipus the King in Three Theban Plays*, trans. by Robert Fagles. London: Penguin.

Stein, M. (1985). Irony in Psychoanalysis. *J. Am. Psychoanal. Assn.*, 33: 35–57.

Steiner, D. (1997). Mutual Admiration between Mother and Baby: A *folie à deux?* In *Female Experience*, eds. J. Raphael-Leff and R. Perelberg. London: Routledge, pp. 163–176.

Steiner, J. (1985). Turning a Blind Eye: The Cover up for Oedipus. *Int. Rev. Psycho-anal.*, 12: 161–172.

Steiner, J. (1990). The Retreat from Truth to Omnipotence in Oedipus at Colonus. *Int. Rev. Psycho-anal.*, 17: 227–237.

Steiner, J. (1993). *Psychic Retreats: Pathological Organisations of the Personality in Psychotic, Neurotic, and Borderline Patients*. London: Routledge.

Steiner, J. (2006). Seeing and Being Seen: Narcissistic Pride and Narcissistic Humiliation. *Int. J. Psychoanal.*, 87: 939–951.

Steiner, J. (2006a). Interpretative Enactments and the Analytic Setting. *Int. J. Psychoanal.*, 87: 315–320.

Steiner, J. (2008). Transference to the Analyst as an Excluded Observer. *Int. J. Psycho-anal.*, 56: 30–43.

Steiner, J. (2011). *Seeing and being Seen: Emerging from a Psychic Retreat*. London: Routledge.

Steiner, J. (2013). The Ideal and the Real in Klein and Milton: Some Observations on Reading Paradise Lost. *Psychoanalytic Quarterly*, 82: 897–923.

Steiner, J. (2015). The Use and Abuse of Omnipotence in the Journey of the Hero. *Psychoanalytic Quarterly*, 84: 695–718.

Steiner, J. (2016). Illusion, Disillusion, and Irony in Psychoanalysis. *Psychoanal. Q.*, 85: 427–447.

Steiner, J. (2017). Introduction, Outline, and Critical Review of Klein's Lectures and Seminars on Technique. In Melanie Klein's Lectures on Technique (1936): Their Relevance for Contemporary Psychoanalysis, ed. M. Klein (2017). Including transcripts of her seminars of 1952. Edited with critical review by J Steiner, Routledge.

Steiner, J. (2018). Overcoming Obstacles in Analysis: Is It Possible to Relinquish Omnipotence and Accept Receptive Femininity? *Psychoanalytic Quarterly*, 87: 1–20.

Steiner, J. (2018a). Time and the Garden of Eden Illusion. *Int. J. Psycho-Anal.*, 99: 1274–1287.

Steiner, J. (2018b). The Trauma and Disillusionment of Oedipus. *Int. J. Psycho-Anal.*, 99: 555–568.

Steiner, J. (2020) Learning from Don Quixote. *Int. J. Psycho-Anal.*, In press.

Stewart, H. (1961). Jocasta's Crimes. *Int. J. Psycho-anal.*, 42: 424–430.

Stoller, R. (1975). Pornography and Perversion. In *Perversion: The Erotic Form of Hatred*. Harvester Press, Chapter 5, pp. 64–91 (Republished by Routledge, London. 2018).

Stoller, R. (1987). Pornography: Daydreams to Cure Humiliation. In *The Many Faces of Shame*, ed. D. L. Nathanson (1987) New York: The Guilford Press, pp. 292–307.

Stoller, R. J. (1979) *Sexual Excitement: Dynamics of Erotic Life*. Pantheon Books. (Kindle Edition, Knopf Doubleday Publishing Group).

Thompson, A. E. (1991). Freud's Pessimism, the Death Instinct, and the Theme of Disintegration in 'Analysis Terminable and Interminable'. *Int. Rev. Psycho-Anal.*, 18: 165–179.

Turri, M. G. (2015). *Transference and Katharsis, Freud to Aristotle. Int.J. Psan*, 96: 369–387.

Vellacott, P. (1971). *Sophocles and Oedipus: A Study of Oedipus Tyrannus with a New Translation*. Ann Arbor, MI: Univ. of Michigan Press.

Vendler, H. (1985). *The Odes of John Keats*. Cambridge, MA: Harvard.

Walsh, J. (2011). Unconscious Dissemblance: The Place of Irony in Psychoanalytic Thought. *PIVOT*, 1: 143–158.

Watling, E. F. (1947). *The Theban Plays*. Harmondsworth: Penguin Books.

Weiss, H. (2008). Romantic Perversion: The Role of Envy in the Creation of a Timeless Universe. In *Envy and Gratitude Revisited*, eds. P. Roth and A. Lemma. London: International Psychoanalytic Association, pp. 152–167.

Weiss, H. (2017). Trauma, Schuldgefühl und Wiedergutmachung. Wie Affekte innere Entwicklung ermöglichen [*Trauma, Guilt and Reparation. How Affects Promote Psychic Development*]. Stuttgart: Klett-Cotta.

Winnicott, D. W. (1953). Transitional Objects and Transitional Phenomena: A Study of the First Not-me Posession. *Int. J Psycho-anal.*, 34: 89–97.

Zepf, S., Ulrich, B., and Seel, D. (2016). Oedipus and the Oedipus Complex: A Revision. *Int. J. Psycho-Anal.*, 97: 685–707.

Zimmerman, S. A. (1981). Milton's Paradise Lost: Eve's Struggle for Identity. *Am. Imago*, 38: 247–267.

Index